1986

S0-AIY-426

GEN 969.4 N548
Newitt, M. D. D.
The Comoro Islands :

3 0301 00094816 2

THE COMORO ISLANDS

PROFILES · NATIONS OF CONTEMPORARY AFRICA
Larry W. Bowman, Series Editor

Also of Interest

THE COMORO ISLANDS

Struggle Against Dependency in the Indian Ocean

Malyn Newitt

LIBRARY
College of St. Francis
JOLIET, ILLINOIS

Westview Press • Boulder, Colorado

Gower • London, England

Profiles / Nations of Contemporary Africa

Unless otherwise noted photographs were taken by the author.

Jacket photographs: (clockwise from top left) police making an arrest at an independence demonstration at Moroni airport in 1973; view of the coast of Mohéli at Niouma Choa; demonstration by the women of the Mouvement Mahorais on Pamanzi Island in 1973.

All rights reserved. No part of this publication may be reproduced or transmitted in any form or by any means, electronic or mechanical, including photocopy, recording, or any information storage and retrieval system, without permission in writing from the publisher.

Copyright © 1984 by Westview Press, Inc.

Published in 1984 in the United States of America by Westview Press, Inc., 5500 Central Avenue, Boulder, Colorado 80301; Frederick A. Praeger, Publisher

Published in 1984 in Great Britain by Gower Publishing Company Limited, Gower House, Croft Road, Aldershot, Hampshire GU11 3HR, England

Library of Congress Cataloging in Publication Data
Newitt, M. D. D.
    The Comoro Islands.
    (Profiles. Nations of contemporary Africa)
    Bibliography: p.
    Includes index.
    1. Comoros. I. Title. II. Series.
DT469.C7N49 1984   969'.4   83-19692
ISBN 0-86531-292-3

British Library Cataloguing in Publication Data
Newitt, Malyn
    The Comoro Islands.—(Nations of
contemporary Africa)
    1. Comoros—Social conditions
    I. Title II. Series
969'.4   HN840.A8
ISBN 0-566-00545-X

Printed and bound in the United States of America

10   9   8   7   6   5   4   3   2   1

969.4
n548

Contents

119,487

Figures, Tables, and Illustrations

Preface

I visited the Comoro Islands in 1973 and spent over two months traveling about the four islands of the archipelago. During that time I met many Comorians who all showed the very warmest hospitality, inviting me to eat in their houses and to attend their festivals and their weddings. It was through talking to them that I learned much about the islands and the way of life and problems of the islanders. It was on this visit also that I met Barbara Dubins and Georges and Geneviève Boulinier. I owe a great deal to all three of them for having been so willing to share with me their expert knowledge of the islands and for having given me so much help in locating some of the less accessible material relating to the Comoros. It was Georges Boulinier who acted as my guide in the ascent of Karthala, who took me to my first *grand mariage*, and who introduced me to a newly caught and deep frozen coelacanth—a trio of experiences that capture perfectly the uniqueness of the islands. His enthusiasm and scholarly interest in the Comoros have made him the best ambassador that these rather forlorn and forgotten communities can have, and I, like so many others, am greatly indebted to him.

I would like also gratefully to acknowledge the expertise of Mike Rouillard, who drew the maps, of Seán Goddard, who designed the cover, and of my sister, Hilary Earl, who prepared the index. I was also given considerable help at every stage of the work by my wife, Joan.

Malyn Newitt

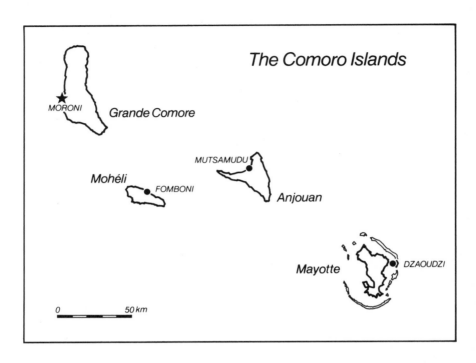

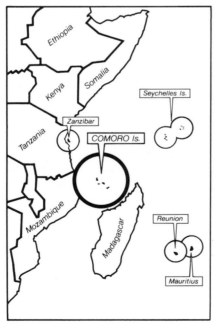

FIGURE 1. The Comoro Islands (above) and FIGURE 2. The Comoro Islands in geographic perspective (left).

1

The Geography of the Islands

POSITION AND CLIMATE

The four islands of the Comoro Archipelago lie between Madagascar and Mozambique in the western Indian Ocean. The inhabitants of the islands know them as Ngazidja, Mwali, Ndzuwani, and Maori. These names are of considerable antiquity and were recorded by Europeans in the early sixteenth century. They were not used by the Portuguese, who gave the islands the names of various saints and navigators, but in a conventionalized form they were adopted by the English and French. The French names for the islands have, in recent years, been the most widely used and have been retained for this book. The French know the islands as Grande Comore, Mohéli, Anjouan, and Mayotte. The name *Comoro* itself appears to come from the Arabic *al-komr*, "the moon," and was originally used to refer to Madagascar before the Portuguese transferred the name to the smaller island group.

The islands lie like a weir across the northern end of the Mozambique Channel. The most westerly is Grande Comore, which is 290 kilometers (181 miles) from the coast of Mozambique. Nearly due south of it at a distance of 45 kilometers (28 miles) is Mohéli (the island that was always known to the English as Mohilla), and 85 kilometers (53 miles) in a southeasterly direction from Grande Comore is Anjouan (the Johanna of English travelers). These three islands are all within sight of one another, although Grande Comore is only visible from Anjouan when certain weather conditions allow the immense dome of the Karthala Volcano to appear as a misty silhouette on the distant horizon. Mayotte, the fourth island, lies 70 kilometers (44 miles) to the southeast of Anjouan. It is the island nearest to Madagascar whose coastline is some 320 kilometers (200 miles) away. Each of the islands has a number of attendant rocks and islets, and when the archipelago was a French colony, the isolated islands of the Mozambique Channel—the Iles Glo-

1

rieuses, Ile St Christophe, Ile de Europa, João da Nova, and the Bassas da India—were administered by France as part of the Comoro Islands territory.

Grande Comore is the largest, highest, and least fertile of the islands. Its 115,000 hectares (444 square miles) are slightly over half the area of the whole archipelago. Anjouan, the second largest island and the most densely populated, is 42,500 hectares (164 square miles), Mayotte is 37,300 hectares (144 square miles), and Mohéli is 29,000 hectares (112 square miles). In all the islands cover 223,800 hectares (864 square miles), which makes them together about the same size as Réunion and a quarter the size of Corsica.

The islands are well within the system of the Indian Ocean monsoons. From April to October is the dry season with winds from the southeast or the southwest but blowing generally from Africa toward the ocean. This is the period of lowest rainfall and lowest temperature. At sea level mean monthly temperatures are around 25° centigrade (77° Fahrenheit), though the continual breezes make the climate appear cooler at this time. The Comorians call the season from April to June *nyombeni*, and during this time, although rain continues to fall, the amount per month can be as low as 0.76 centimeters (0.3 inches) on Mayotte, 1.44 centimeters (0.6 inches) in the north of Grande Comore, and 3.81 centimeters (1.5 inches) on Mohéli during May.

The season from July to October is called *kusi* and is the time when the weather gets hotter and the air more humid. The high mountains now hold the clouds, which causes frequent showers, and only in the early morning can the high peaks of Karthala and N'Tingui be seen quite free from vapor before sea breezes blow up fresh clouds to envelop them.

Toward the end of October the northeast monsoon begins to blow. There have usually been signs of a change of weather; rainfall has been more frequent and the days hotter with some moments of suffocating, ovenlike heat. With the change to the monsoon begins the season called *kachi-kazi*. The rain falls in torrents reaching peaks in January when 33.5 centimeters (13.2 inches) in Mayotte, 38.35 centimeters (15.1 inches) in Anjouan, and 24.89 centimeters (9.8 inches) in Mohéli and Grande Comore are not uncommon at sea level. A thousand meters up the mountains the rainfall can be astonishingly heavy. At Boboni on Grande Comore, where there was once a sawmill for exploiting the timber of the rain forest, the annual rainfall can be as much as 541 centimeters (213 inches), more than twice the annual amount on the coast. Cyclones, a further hazard of the wet season, blow up from the east, veer northwards, and can strike any of the islands from December onward. The effects of the cyclones on the forests and plantations of the islands can be devastating, but fortunately they occur only at irregular intervals. During the wet season average daytime temperatures at sea level can rise to 28° or 29° centigrade (82° or 84° Fahrenheit).[1]

Although the islands are small, considerable variations exist in their climates. The high mountains of Grande Comore and Anjouan create rain shadows, so that one can cross from luxuriant vegetation on Anjouan's northern coast to dry savannah in the east in a matter of only half an hour's drive. Similar changes can be found in the ascent of Karthala as one passes from the palm and banana belt of the coast to the rain forest and then on to the summit, which is dry, cold, and colonized by heaths and other temperate plants.

In spite of the very heavy rainfall in the islands, the availability of water has always been a crucial factor in their human and natural geography. Mayotte and Mohéli are well supplied with running water, and Anjouan has perennial streams that flow from the central mountain peak of N'Tingui, but the three peninsulas of Anjouan and the whole of Grande Comore are completely lacking in running water. Grande Comore has no geological formation that will hold water, and although five meters (16.41 feet) or more of rain may fall on the slopes of Karthala annually, within two or three weeks of the end of the rains all the water courses are dry. Traditionally the inhabitants have depended on rainwater tanks and cisterns, or they have dug wells on the seashore into which seawater will filter.[2] The French made a number of attempts to find a subterranean supply of water, but only in 1976 was a satisfactory deep well bored south of Moroni from which the capital at least could be supplied.

GEOLOGICAL FORMATION OF THE ISLANDS

The four Comoro islands and their satellite islets have been entirely formed by volcanic action occurring along a fissure running west-north-west to east-south-east.[3] The volcanic action that formed the island of Mayotte took place in Miocene times. Since the formation of the island the level of the sea has risen, and this, coupled with heavy erosion, has given Mayotte a rugged and indented coastline, the surrounding shallows studded with numerous rocks and islands. Mayotte is largely surrounded by a barrier reef that lies from 3 kilometers (1.87 miles) to 15 kilometers (9.37 miles) from the shore with breaches in the north and east caused by the runoff of fresh water from the island.

Off the northeast coast of Mayotte lies the island of Pamanzi on which is a large crater lake called Dziani. This and other ash cones on the main island are signs of more recent volcanic rejuvenation, but Pamanzi has also the curious feature of seabed deposits high up near the rim of the crater, which can only be explained in terms of a raising of the seabed when the crater was formed. Pamanzi is linked by shallows with other small islands in the bay of Mamoutzou and by a causeway with the waterless rock of Dzaoudzi, where the French built their administrative headquarters in the nineteenth century, planning to turn it into the "Gibraltar" of the Indian Ocean.

4

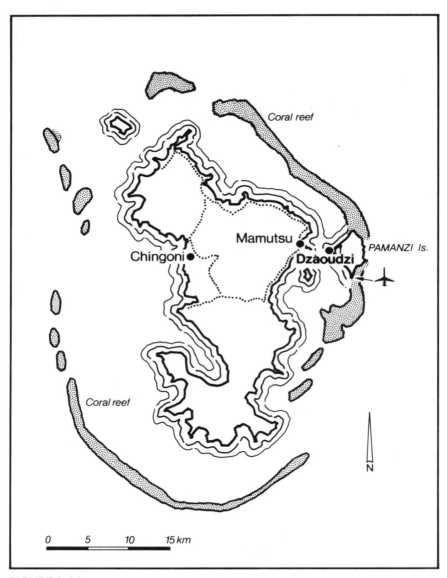

FIGURE 3. Mayotte

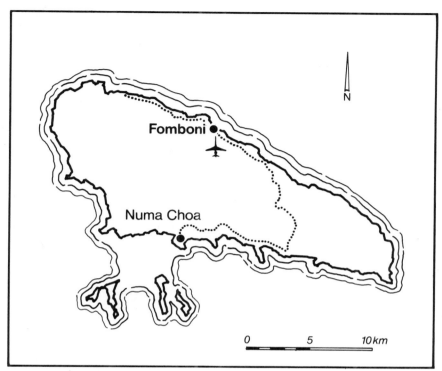

FIGURE 4. Mohéli

The highest land in Mayotte is 660 meters (2,166 feet), but the most striking feature is Outchongui, a bare and abrupt sugarloaf mountain in the south of the island that for centuries was the most familiar landmark for storm-bound ships in the Mozambique Channel. The rest of the island has a broken and uneven surface largely covered by secondary forest and scrubby bush. The coasts are fringed with mangroves, which grow thickly under the protection provided by the reefs. All the main centers of population are on the coast, and only a quarter of all the Mahorais live inland. There is no town of any size on the island, and the only urban services that exist are in the area of Dzaoudzi and Pamanzi, where the French maintain an administration.

Mohéli and Anjouan[4] are younger in geological age, although neither have a record of volcanic activity in historic times. The first phase of volcanic activity on Anjouan raised a great shield volcano, the scarred remains of which form the central peak of N'Tingui, which rises to 1,595 meters (5,235 feet). The second phase of activity occurred around the central volcano and led to the formation of the peninsulas that make up the triangular shape of the island. A final third phase appears to have been highly explosive and left the face of the island

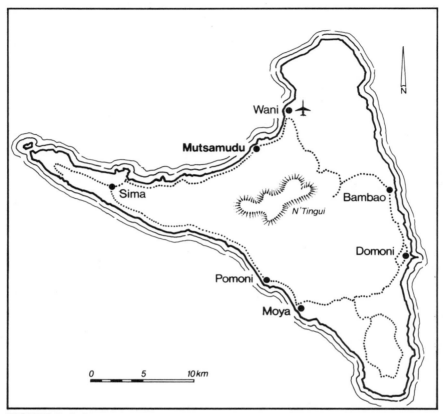

FIGURE 5. Anjouan

pitted with ash cones. Today Anjouan presents from every side a most majestic outline of mountain ranges cut by valleys and deep gorges that give it an almost alpine appearance. The mountain peaks, although in many places precipitous, are all clothed with thick forest and are frequently enveloped in clouds. Behind the main peak lies a little crater lake called Dzialandze and beneath opens out the great amphitheater of Bambao that gives Anjouan its largest and most fertile flatlands. Water from the mountains operates a small hydroelectric station at the head of the valley.

Mohéli also shows signs of having originated in a great central volcano, the original outline of which is indicated by the long straggling islands that lie off the south coast. However, there have been more recent lava flows from fissures, and the island is dotted with ash cones. Apart from the coastal plain in the north, most of the island is thickly wooded and mountainous, though without any outstanding mountain peaks. Some 85 percent of the population lives on the coast, and parts of the interior are nearly deserted. On the south coast the mountains slope down to the sea, which is studded with islands and fringed by miles of magnificent sand presenting some of the finest and wildest scenery of the archipelago.

Grande Comore is the youngest of the islands and its main volcano is still very active. The island is formed by two large domed shield volcanoes: Karthala, which is 2,400 meters (7,877 feet) and La Grille, which is just over 1,000 meters (3,282 feet). In the far south is the mountain massif of Mbadjini. There has been no volcanic activity from La Grille's summit in historic times, although there are comparatively young lava flows originating from fissures in its sides and the whole of the mountain is studded with ash cones, many of them so abrupt and clear-cut that the flanks of the mountain have been compared to a lunar landscape.

Karthala[5] has shown considerable activity in modern times, although only one of its eruptions, that of 1965, has been properly studied. Most of the flows of lava that scar the sides of the mountain have issued from fissures more or less near the summit, and between 1857 and 1862 there were five such major eruptions. One of these sent a stream of lava between the towns of Itsandra and Moroni and completely destroyed a large village that lay above them. There were further eruptions in 1872, 1880, and 1904. In 1918 the first eruption to be described in any detail occurred. Since then all activity has been confined to the summit, with a major eruption in 1945 and others in 1952, 1965, and 1977.

Karthala is a gently rounded, domelike mountain with no striking feature except its massive bulk, which dominates every aspect of the island. Its summit has collapsed inward to form one of the largest calderas of any of the world's active volcanoes. As it appears today the caldera measures four kilometers (2.5 miles) in one direction and three kilometers (1.87 miles) in the other. Its walls are about 100 meters (328 feet) high with one large breach toward the north, called the porte d'Itsandre, where lava flows have cut a passage.

Within the caldera are two pit craters. The largest is Chahale which measures 1,300 meters (4,267 feet) by 800 meters (2,600 feet) and is 200–300 meters (650–1,000 feet) deep. The other crater is smaller and lies to the south. It is called Changoumeni and has been the scene of much of the modern activity of the volcano. Changoumeni has some fumarole activity and lies gently smoking even when the mountain itself is quiescent.

Because Grande Comore is geologically so young, it has not eroded or worn into valleys and peaks like the other islands. The mountains slope evenly into the sea, and there is only a narrow coastal plain on the western side where gardens and plantations are possible. The most striking features of the island's landscape are the lava flows, which have

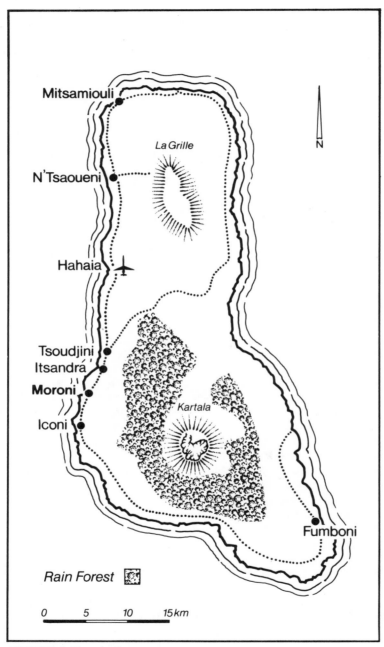

Mitsamiouli

La Grille

N'Tsaoueni

Hahaia

Tsoudjini
Itsandra
Moroni
Iconi

Kartala

Fumboni

N

Rain Forest

0   5   10   15 km

FIGURE 6. Grande Comore

burnt their way through the forests like great black glaciers and have poured into the sea leaving a dark, craggy shoreline. Karthala itself is covered with rain forest, but the road that crosses the waist of the island between the two volcanoes passes through open grasslands extensively used for cattle grazing. The overwhelming majority of the population lives, and has always lived, on the western side of the island where all the major towns are to be found. Fumboni in the extreme southeast is the only important exception.

SOIL AND VEGETATION

The soils of the islands are made up of laterite in a greater or lesser degree of decay. They are rich in some minerals but in general lack humus and need careful husbandry if they are to prove fertile. The soils have not received enough care from either French planters or Comorian peasants, and they have shown a tendency to rapid exhaustion. The steep mountainsides make erosion a problem that is already far advanced, particularly in Anjouan. Grande Comore has very little topsoil at all, and large parts of the island's surface consist of bare rock, which somehow provides sustenance for ferns and trees but not for arable crops. As in many parts of the world, the luxuriance of tropical vegetation disguises basically poor soil—a fact that is ruthlessly exposed once the forest is destroyed.

The Comoro Islands were at one time largely covered by primary evergreen rain forest.[6] However, parts of the archipelago have always had a different type of vegetation altogether. Mayotte has less than half the average rainfall of the mountains of Grande Comore, and parts of it, for instance Pamanzi Island, together with the drier areas of eastern Anjouan and Grande Comore have an open type of savannah characterized by low trees, bushes, and baobabs. The summit of Karthala is different again, being covered with giant *Philippia comorensis*—heather trees that grow right up to the rim of the caldera and even colonize the interior until they are burnt back by an eruption.

The rain forest has been severely damaged by human occupation and continues to dwindle. On Anjouan the only extensive area of forest left is that which clothes the high central peak of N'Tingui, which is too steep for cultivation. Even where rain forest still stands, its continued survival is in doubt because of the local farmers' habit of stripping the undergrowth to grow bananas while leaving the canopy intact.

On Mayotte the primary forest has almost all disappeared. To the damage caused by the agriculture of the indigenous inhabitants must be added the results of the invasion of French sugar planters who cleared much of the best land for their crops. The local farmers were forced into the forests where many of them took to a kind of shifting cultivation, burning off tracts of forest for a single season's crops. Today there is only one patch of forest left around Outchongui Mountain in the south of the island, although the abandonment of the sugar plantations has allowed a shaggy, secondary scrub to recolonize the land, giving much of it a forlorn and rather desolate appearance. The sugar planters also brought about the draining of the alluvial marshes that were a feature of Mayotte on their arrival.

On Mohéli and Grande Comore the forest is less damaged. The small population of Mohéli lives near the coast, and the interior of the island is still heavily wooded. Grande Comore retains some magnificent stands of rain forest on the slopes of the Karthala Volcano. Most of this lies above the 600 meter (1,969 foot) line, but the western side of the mountain has, in general, been more severely affected by the French timber companies and the banana farmers than the largely untouched south and east sides. The Karthala rain forest is still one of the greatest natural resources of the archipelago. Besides being a source of quantities of large timber, it plays a crucial role in attracting and holding moisture. There would not be much gain from further destruction of the forest, for its luxuriant growth is founded not on a fertile soil but on the rocky lava flows of the mountainside. However, the felling of the forest appears to be continuing with little restraint.

The flora of the Comoros, like the fauna, is closely related to that of Madagascar and owes more to that island than to Africa. At the same time it is poorer in indigenous species than either. The timber trees exploited by the French companies include *Eugenia, khaya, Lasiodiscus, macaranga, Ocotea,* and *Weinmania;* and local craftsmen use the mango, the breadfruit, the *badamier,* and the *albizzia* for the construction of canoes and the red-brown *takamaka* for making furniture and doors and for wood carving.

The rain forest of Grande Comore is rich in ferns (*Cyathea similis*), mosses, lianas, and orchids (*Angraecum eburneum, Jumellea oberonia disticha, Cynosorchis galatea, Disperis comorensis*) but not in palms. The lowlands of Mayotte also have massive stands of bamboo, which are extensively used in building, and mangrove swamps along the coasts. Both of these are rare on the other three islands.

A large part of the flora of the archipelago has been introduced by human agency. Of the thirty-three main food crops, seventeen are of East Asian origin, eleven derive from the Americas, three from the Mediterranean or Near East, and one each come from West Africa and Ethiopia.[7] To these must be added the crops specific to the plantation economy, introduced in the last hundred years, which include cloves, cinnamon, vanilla, cashew, cacao, coffee, sisal, and a variety of scent-producing plants, the most important of which is ylang-ylang, whose twisted, vinelike forms are such a common sight in the islands. The commercial fortunes of these plantation crops have varied, but even when, like coffee, they have largely failed or, like sisal, have been discontinued altogether, their relics still contribute to the variety of the islands' flora.

The three crops most commonly cultivated by the Comorians themselves are cassava, coconut, and banana. These are lowland plants and produce the lightly wooded, shady landscape so familiar in the coastal regions of the archipelago. Peppers, oranges, pawpaws, tomatoes, and onions are also commonly grown, as is rice on Anjouan. However, these are usually grown for home consumption, and the quality is often poor. Looking at the poverty of a modern Comorian market it is sometimes difficult to understand that the islands once had a reputation as a refreshment station, producing large surpluses of tropical foodstuffs for international shipping. One of the most attractive fruits that grows in the islands is what the French inaccurately describe as *framboise*. They grow in the mountains at about 300 meters (1,000 feet) and are, in fact, the berries of a bramble (*Rubus rosaeflorus*). On Anjouan, children market the berries in little punnets woven from palm leaves, but on Grande Comore they seem to be left unpicked. Also common are kapok trees that in August and September stand leafless and hung with pods spilling out their wooly contents.

FAUNA

Like the flora of the Comoros, the fauna is poor in species and seems to be a zoological satellite of Madagascar rather than Africa— although, as might be expected, the influence of Africa is stronger on the western side of the archipelago.[8] Unlike the Seychelles and Mascarene Islands, the Comoros have had a human population for a thousand years at the very least. The land fauna has not, therefore, enjoyed the isolation that would have led to the survival or evolution of unique species.

There are some 832 insect species recorded in the Comoros, 283 of which are said to be endemic. Ants are rare and driver ants are unknown, but mosquitoes, especially those carrying malaria and elephantiasis, are only too common, as travelers soon discover. So, too, are spiders, which number among their fraternity one of large proportions that spins a massive web, sometimes spanning a whole pathway, and that can colonize and cocoon an empty house in a short time. There are lizards but no snakes.

Lemurs of two kinds are found on Mayotte and Anjouan—the *mongoz* lemur, which is also found in Madagascar, and the *macaco*, which is endemic to Mayotte. This latter is the chief claim that the Comoros have to any fame in the animal world. The male is black and grows to about two and a half feet; the female is reddish in color. They live in small troops and are protected both by French law and by local tradition. There is a shrew (*Suncus coqueeli*) that is also endemic to Mayotte and a chameleon (*Chamaeleo polleni*) that possibly is, and the fact that these endemic species are all found on Mayotte may suggest to the expert some clue to the geological evolution of the archipelago.

Bats are extremely common and are treated as vermin, but like all vermin, they thrive; and the trees around the villages are hung during the day with the black, cobweblike fruit bats (*Pterops comorensis*). In the evening they can be seen wheeling far out to sea like vampire gulls. Among the animals that have been introduced and become indigenized are the tenrec (*Tenrec ecaudatus*), a wild cat (*Felis lybica caffra*), and the Madagascar wild pig. Wild cattle are said to exist in the forest of Grande Comore. Domesticated animals include hens, sheep, goats, and humped zebu-type cattle, usually quite small in size. As the population is almost entirely Muslim, however, pigs and dogs are virtually unknown. Donkeys are used domestically on all the islands except Grande Comore, where the rocky ground destroys their feet. Rats and mice have become a major problem, attacking food stores and domestic fowls, and a campaign to rid the islands of these pests is now crucial.

The birds of the Comoros have been studied scientifically since 1843 when the explorer and ornithologist Wilhelm Peters visited Anjouan. By 1908 all the main species and subspecies had been identified, but further study of migration, habitats, and breeding was made by the British Ornithological Union in 1958.[9] The only genus endemic to the Comoros is Humblot's flycatcher (*Humblotia flavirostris*), named after the French naturalist and entrepreneur Léon Humblot. The bird only breeds in Grande Comore. In addition, there are nine endemic species, and this small number indicates that in general the Comoros are not rich in bird life. The forested mountain slopes of Karthala, in fact, contain only half the number of species to be found in similar habitats in Malawi and on Madagascar. One reason for this might be that the clearing of the forests has severely disturbed the habitats of many birds, but against this should be set the fact that in the Comoros birds have few predators and, with the exception of the luckless pigeons, are seldom hunted. Moreover, on Anjouan, which is the most densely populated island and where the forest has been severely damaged, there are the same number of species as on Grande Comore.

In all, fifty-six bird species nest on the island; twenty-nine are related to the birds of Madagascar, only twelve to those of Africa, and seven are related to both. As the islands are equidistant from Africa and Madagascar, the predominance of types from the latter is significant but clearly matches the same tendency among the other land fauna.

The fame of the Comoros in the zoological world rests with the discoveries that have been made in the seas off the islands. Grande Comore and Anjouan are, on the whole, poor in marine life, as the sea slopes steeply away from the shore. Mohéli, however, has stretches of coral reef, and Mayotte is almost surrounded by a large barrier reef that is still alive and remains largely unpolluted. The riches of the Mayotte reef have been the subject of monographs and films, but it was not on the reef that the discovery was made that turned the Comoros into the center of attraction for ichthyologists from all over the world. Indeed, the discovery was not actually made in the Comoros at all.

In 1938 the director of the East London Museum was brought a strange fish that had been trawled off the South African coast.[10] The fish was soon identified as being closely related to the freshwater coelacanth that had been thought extinct for 50 million years. It was not until 1952, however, that the search for a second coelacanth was rewarded, and it was discovered that the breeding ground and natural habitat of the fish was off the Comoros. Since 1952 coelacanths have been caught in increasing numbers, though only in the waters off Anjouan and Grande Comore. They live at considerable depths, and the process of bringing them to the surface ensures that they will not survive captivity. As a result, no coelacanth has been extensively studied while still alive.

Competition to secure specimens has meant that growing numbers of the fish have been caught. As little is known about the size of the coelacanth's population or about its breeding habits, there must be a severe risk that this remarkable creature will be hunted to extinction—a fate that has already overtaken the dodo of Mauritius and seems in store for the tortoises of Aldabra.

Compared with many African countries, the Comoros are very well endowed by nature. Their soil has great natural fertility and they have a pleasant climate and more than adequate rainfall. Indeed, in the days of sailing ships, the islands enjoyed a high reputation for the richness and variety of their produce. However, as with many islands, the smallness of the land area leaves the ecology precariously balanced. Destruction of the forests, soil erosion, and the pollution of the coastal waters are threatening to destroy the habitats of many plant and animal species. However, the greatest threat of all is coming from the too rapidly increasing human population. Because the islands are so small it is possible to see in a particularly striking manner the consequences of man failing to live within the limits of his natural environment.

NOTES

1. For the climate of the Comoros see, among others, H. Isnard, "L'Archipel des Comores," *Les cahiers d'outre-mer* 21 (1953), pp. 5–6; and Claude Robineau, *Société et économie d'Anjouan* (Paris: ORSTOM, 1966), pp. 24–25.

2. The seawater wells, which can still be seen today, were described as early as 1608 by Alexander Sharpey. See extract in A. Grandidier and G. Grandidier, eds., *Collection des ouvrages anciens concernant Madagascar* (hereafter *COACM*), 9 vols. (Paris, 1903–1920), vol. 1, pp. 418–421. For a more recent description see Nicolas Du Plantier, *La Grande Comore* (Paris, 1904), p. 10.

3. J. Esson, M. Flower, D. Strong, B. Lupton, and W. Wadsworth, "Geology of the Comores Archipelago, Western Indian Ocean," *Geological Magazine* 107 (1970), pp. 549–557, and works cited therein.

4. For the geology of Anjouan see also J. Tricart, "Reconnaissance géomorphologique de l'Ile de Anjouan," *Madagascar: Revue de géographie*, July–December 1972, pp. 79–107.

5. For a description of the volcano see D. Strong and F. Jacquot, "The Karthala Caldera, Grande Comore," *Bulletin Volcanologique* 34 (1971), pp. 663–680. The most extensive bibliography on the volcano is in G. Boulinier and G. Boulinier-Giraud, "Volcanisme et traditions populaires à la Grande Comore," *Asie du sud-est et monde insulindien* 7 (1976), pp. 45–71.

6. The best introduction to the flora and fauna of the Comoros is in C. W. Benson, "The Birds of the Comoro Islands," *Ibis* 103b (1960), pp. 55–106.

7. Robineau, *Société et économie d'Anjouan*, p. 26.

8. For the fauna see Benson, "Birds of the Comoro Islands"; and Franco Prosperi, *A Vanished Continent* (London: Hutchinson, 1957). A specialist bibliography on the fauna can be found in Jean Gorse, *Territoire des Comores: Bibliographie* (Paris: BDPA, 1964), pp. 26–28, cyclostyled.

9. Benson, "Birds of the Comoro Islands."

10. For an account of the discovery of the coelacanth see J.L.B. Smith, *Old Fourlegs; The Story of the Coelacanth* (London: Pan Books, 1958); also D. E. McAllister, *Old Fourlegs: A Living Fossil* (Ottawa: National Museum of Natural Sciences, 1971).

2

The History of
the Comoro Islands

THE MUSLIM SETTLEMENT

The Comoro Islands form a natural series of stepping-stones between Africa and Madagascar and have almost certainly been the main migration route between the two for humans as they have for animals and birds. For example, the Indonesian immigrants, the ancestors of the Merina population of Madagascar, probably reached that island via East Africa, in which case they would have used the Comoros as a migration route and may have established the first human settlements in the archipelago sometime in the first millennium A.D.[1] Indonesians were followed by Africans from central Africa and by Islamic traders who began to extend their commercial empire down the coast of eastern Africa in about the twelfth century, exporting gold, ivory, and other luxury commodities to the Gulf and to India.

The most important Muslim trading state was Kilwa on the coast of modern-day Tanzania. From there many Islamic settlements were founded, which participated in coastal trade and supplied the larger cities with foodstuffs, timber, gum, coir, and other local products. It was natural that a trade route should develop from Kilwa southeast through the Comoros, and Muslim towns grew up around the northern end of Madagascar at Vohémar, Langane, Sada, and elsewhere. These towns built up an important commerce in palm cloth, timber, and rice, and a rather specialized export of carved stone containers.[2] The Comoro Islands became regular stopping places for ships passing from Kilwa to Madagascar, and it is in this context that they are first clearly mentioned by a contemporary writer. In a guide written for sailors in the Indian Ocean at the end of the fifteenth century, the distinguished Arab navigator, Ahmed ibn Majid, mentions the town of Domoni on Anjouan and refers to the islands generally as "places where people buy and sell."[3] Four years later a Portuguese captain attached to the fleet of Tristan da Cunha

15

visited the islands and reported, "there are many provisions in the islands of Alcomor, millet, rice, cows, goats, hens . . . and from there Kilwa and Mombasa are supplied."[4]

The population of the islands, therefore, was built up by the passage of migrants and traders between the African mainland and Madagascar and, no doubt, by the slaves they brought with them. At some stage, however, a number of prestigious Muslim clans made homes in the archipelago. The Muslims described themselves in their traditional histories as "Shirazi," which suggests that they recognized a close connection with the so-called Shirazi families of Kilwa and Zanzibar. Their settlement in the islands may extend back to the thirteenth century, but it is more likely that most of them settled in the islands after the sack of Kilwa by the Portuguese in 1506. They continued to maintain close contacts with the ruling families of the Swahili coast of Africa, with whom they intermarried and conducted trade.[5]

The Shirazi are associated in the traditional histories with the spread of Islam and the building of mosques, and up to the present, the ruling families have been at pains to keep close religious ties with the centers of the Islamic world.[6] The Shirazi were also revered as the founders of towns, and a number of the historic urban centers of the Comoros are especially associated with them—for example, Chingoni on Mayotte and the now deserted town of Sima on Anjouan. The Shirazi clearly sought to recreate the coastal city-state, which was the principal Islamic political unit in eastern Africa. They did not seek, however, to bring the islands under a common sovereignty and certainly did not succeed in doing so. The Portuguese record that in the middle of the sixteenth century there were twenty separate chieftaincies on Grande Comore. The traditional histories of the islands stress the rivalry between the different cities—for instance, between Sima and Domoni (and later Mutsammudu) on Anjouan and between Chingoni and Qualey on Mayotte. The failure of the Muslim urban rulers to establish some form of unified government was also partly due to the fact that the indigenous inhabitants resisted being absorbed and retained a large degree of independence in the interior of the islands under the rule of their own chiefs (called *fanis* on Anjouan and *fey* or *beja* on Grande Comore). All early accounts of the islands stress the ethnic differences in the population. João de Castro, writing in the 1540s, refers to the islanders as "blacks" and then says, "along the seashore live some moors."[7] A similar distinction is made by the Dominican João dos Santos, at the end of the century. The traditional histories stress the marriage alliances made by the Shirazi with the chiefs they found in the islands, and this suggests also that the newcomers found it wisest to cohabit with the established population rather than seek to dominate it.

The traditional histories remember the sixteenth century as a period of considerable prosperity, and it may be that the three smaller islands did come, for a brief period, under the rule of a single sultan, for the

ruling clans certainly established a hierarchy of prestige among themselves. The Portuguese, who sought to impose a trade monopoly throughout the Indian Ocean, made no serious attempt to occupy the Comoros,
but their settlers on Mozambique Island did come to rely on the islands
for food supplies and traded regularly with them. The Comoros also
gained something of a position for themselves in international trade.
Some Muslim commerce did manage to evade the Portuguese monopoly,
and the towns on Madagascar and the Comoros, as they were not
occupied by Portugal, assumed a relatively more important role in
international commerce. A report from 1614 speaks of Anjouan importing
opium and cotton cloth from the Red Sea area and exporting rice,
ambergris, and slaves. The Portuguese also record a considerable trade
in spices with the Gulf. By the early seventeenth century slaves had
become the major item of commerce—their destination not European
or American markets, but the Islamic ports of the northern part of the
Indian Ocean.[8]

In the 1590s the first serious European challenge to the Portuguese
appeared, and the Comoros began to be at the center of a bitter struggle
for maritime supremacy between the rival European trading nations.

EUROPEAN TRADING COMPANIES

The English East India Company was founded in 1601 and its
Dutch counterpart in 1602. The first French *Compagnie des Indes* was
not established until 1664, but from early in the century French trading
ships regularly sailed for the East. The northern Europeans, in order to
avoid having to stop at places occupied by the Portuguese, called regularly
at the Comoros in search of fresh water and provisions. Eventually they
were all to establish intermediate bases of their own, the English
occupying St. Helena in 1651, the French establishing a colony in
Madagascar, and the Dutch settling in Mauritius and at the Cape of
Good Hope. However, the Comoros remained a most important port
of call throughout the seventeenth and eighteenth centuries for all three
nations. French, English, and Dutch squadrons visited the islands and
bought provisions. They also left letters, landed sick seamen, and picked
up those left behind by previous ships. The islands inevitably became
involved in the endemic warfare waged by the three nations against
the Portuguese in the Mozambique Channel. The Dutch, for example,
used Mayotte as a base from which to launch their attacks on Mozambique
Island in 1607 and 1608, and some major naval actions were fought
off the islands.[9] The most dramatic of these was probably the attack
by four English warships on the carrack carrying the Portuguese viceroy,
Dom Manuel de Meneses, to Goa in 1616. The carrack was eventually
dismasted, and it ran aground on Grande Comore, where it was burnt.

These regular visits by individual European ships, and sometimes
by whole fleets, had a profound effect on the economic development

of the islands. The ships purchased large quantities of foodstuffs, buying up whole herds of cattle and frequently taking everything that was on offer. In 1607, for example, Van Caerden bought 366 head of cattle and 276 goats in Mayotte to supply his fleet; in 1617 Edward Monox was told that he could ship 30 head of cattle at once and the full 100 he was requesting if he could wait a day; and in 1634 Richard Allnutt bought 79 head of cattle and 27 goats on Anjouan.[10] Demands of this kind certainly stimulated food production and trade between the islands, since cattle and other commodities were shipped from the less favored ports and islands for sale at the points where European ships were calling. There is some evidence that this increased demand for food encouraged the ruling Muslim families to increase their control over the interior of the islands and to introduce slaves for cultivation. They thus became increasingly a landowning as well as a commercial class. The island sultans also seem to have attempted to control the markets and prices of goods—though this may have been in order to keep prices down, for European captains continued to think of the Comoro foodstuffs as cheap.

The visits of European vessels also had a considerable political impact, for the captains came to prefer certain anchorages to others and called at these regularly. In the early days all the islands had been visited, but European ships soon began to avoid Grande Comore altogether. Their behavior was always attributed to the hostility of the local inhabitants who had murdered some of the crew of Sir James Lancaster's ship in 1591. The real reason, however, was that Grande Comore had no good anchorages and lacked fresh water, a commodity much in demand by sailing ships. Conversely, Mutsammudu on Anjouan, lying on a wide and sheltered bay (on which also stood the old walled town of Wani), soon rose to prominence. Its hinterland was fertile, and its greatest asset was the river that entered the sea near the town and was visited and described by generations of grateful seamen.

There is a similar pattern of development for the other islands. Mayotte gradually dropped out of favor, partly because of the dangers presented by its reef but also because it became a haunt of pirates. Mohéli, on the other hand, remained popular. European ships anchored in the open roadstead off Fomboni, and gradually this town grew in importance, overshadowing Niouma Choa on the other side of the island.

In this way visiting ships conferred their favors on one town and one island rather than another, inevitably increasing the wealth and political importance of those they visited at the expense of less favored rivals. The policy of the English East India Company was to keep out of local quarrels, but it was also company policy to retain the friendship and cooperation of the rulers in the ports they visited. Ultimately these two lines of policy were irreconcilable, for the very act of trading with one party strengthened its position in the political world of the archipelago. Much of the trade with European vessels was carried out in coin or through the purchase of luxuries, among which paper was much in demand. However, the staple of the trade was always metal, for the islands had no ore deposits and had to import iron and metal objects of all kinds. European visitors recorded that the imported iron was frequently worked into weapons and that items such as sword blades fetched high prices.[11]

During the seventeenth century the political rivalries of the Comorians became increasingly violent. Armed in whatever way they could manage, sometimes only with sticks and stones, the islanders launched attacks on each other and plundered and burnt each other's towns. The causes of these endless raids are obscure. Clan rivalries undoubtedly ran deep and were exacerbated by the favor shown by European ships to one port over another. The Almassella clan of Mutsammudu, for example, not only rose to prominence at the expense of the Almadua of Domoni but also managed to gain recognition from the English East India Company of their paramountcy over the old seat of Shirazi power. The raids were also, apparently, stimulated by the growing trade in slaves, which remained the most important commodity traded by the islanders with the Islamic world.

Although officially enjoined to keep out these troubles, the visiting European captains found themselves besieged with requests for arms and help with transport across the sea and with pleas for protection. Protection, at least, was hard to refuse if the supply of provisions was to continue. Recognizing this, the English East India Company increasingly granted its special protection to the Almassella sultans of Mutsammudu. The most striking example of this protection occurred in the 1770s when marines from a visiting company ship helped the sultan to suppress a dangerous servile revolt, led by Tumpa, that had broken out in the interior.[12] Other European ships also lent their aid, more or less discreetly, to their particular protégés.

PIRACY

Europeans were undoubtedly influenced to take a more active part in the affairs of the archipelago by the growth of piracy and privateering in the region. In the first half of the seventeenth century there were some clashes between English ships working out the rivalries of the Civil War or challenging the monopoly of the English East India Company. However, the real growth of piracy took place in the second half of the century when improved security in the Caribbean persuaded many former buccaneers to switch their activities to the Indian Ocean and to set up bases on the northeast coast of Madagascar. The Mozambique Channel became one of their favorite cruising grounds. The pirate ships would lie in wait along the coasts of the Comoros, and they frequently used the comparative safety of the Mayotte lagoon to careen or to take on water. In the bazaars of the island ports they picked up information

about the movement of company ships, and Captain Cornwall warned
all vessels visiting Anjouan "to be very cautious of mentioning whither
they are bound, by Reason the European pirates repair hither constantly,
to learn what ships are in those seas, their strength, loading and Port
destined to."[13] The pirates would also frequently sell plundered property
on the islands.

The sultans of the Comoros remained on good terms with the
pirates, for they needed their protection and were willing to trade with
all comers. However, their neutral stance became difficult as the English
East India Company stepped up its war on the pirates with the cooperation
of the French who established themselves on the former Dutch island
of Mauritius in 1710. As the islands became less secure as bases, the
pirates began to see them as targets for attack and plunder. In 1701,
for example, the notorious pirate, Captain North, plundered the coast
of Grande Comore and then attacked Mayotte and took the sultan
prisoner, obtaining for him a ransom, which was paid in silver chains.[14]
A number of engagements took place off the islands between pirates
and company ships. Perhaps the most dramatic of these was the fight
between the *Cassandra* and two large pirate ships off Anjouan in 1720.
Captain Mackra of the *Cassandra* eventually had to abandon ship. He
fled ashore and lived to accuse his two companions who had put out
to sea rather than stand by him and fight.[15]

The suppression of piracy had the effect of involving both the
French and the English more deeply in the politics of the region. French
cruisers from Ile de France (as Mauritius had been renamed) regularly
visited the coast of Madagascar, while the English strengthened their
links with Anjouan until it became virtually an English East India
Company protectorate. Under the possessive eye of the company, Mutsammudu became the commercial center of the archipelago. Sir William
Jones, who visited Anjouan in 1783, records a conversation with a
member of the ruling family:

> His country, he said, was poor, and produced few articles for trade; but
> if they could get money, *which they now preferred to playthings* . . . they
> might easilly procure foreign commodities and exchange them advanta-
> geously with their neighbours in the islands and on the continent. Thus
> with a little money, he said, we purchase muskets, powder, balls, cutlasses,
> knives, clothes, raw cotton, and other articles brought from Bombay, and
> with those we trade to *Madagascar* for the natural produce of the country
> for *dollars*, with which the *French* buy cattle, honey, butter and so forth,
> in that island. With *gold*, which we receive from your ships, we can
> procure elephants teeth from the natives of Mozambique, who barter them
> also for ammunition and bars of iron; and the *Portuguese* in that country
> give us cloths of various kinds in exchange for our commodities; these
> cloths we dispose of lucratively in the three neighbouring islands, whence
> we bring rice, cattle, a kind of breadfruit, which grows in *Comora*, and
> *slaves* which we buy also at other places to which we trade; and we carry
> on this traffic in our own vessels.[16]

This passage reads rather like a homily on the virtues of free trade, but it no doubt records fairly accurately the complexity of the trading network at the center of which Mutsammudu and its ruling clans found themselves at the end of the eighteenth century. Grande Comore, Mayotte, and Mohéli still retained some coastal trade and kept their important links with the Swahili cities of East Africa, but the first two were seldom visited by Europeans and Mohéli was subject to the more or less permanent overlordship of Anjoun.

CIVIL WAR AND MALAGASY INTERVENTION

Between 1780 and 1840 the Comoro Islands experienced almost continuous civil war, war that became inextricably entangled with the struggle for power in neighboring Madagascar. The background to this strife lay in the major economic changes that affected the whole Indian Ocean in the eighteenth century.

As has been shown already, the Comoros were involved in two interlocking trade systems: one with European trading companies, the other with the Islamic mercantile community of the western Indian Ocean that used the islands as a clearinghouse for a variety of commodities but especially for the export of slaves from Madagascar. By the middle of the eighteenth century the French settlers in Ile de France had begun to establish plantations, which added a whole new dimension to the trade of the region. As a result of their successful ventures, the French also settled in the hitherto uncolonized Seychelles. The demand for plantation labor grew in a spectacular fashion, and the slave trade, with its massive speculative profits, soon outpaced other forms of commercial activity in the whole western region of the Indian Ocean. Between 1769 and 1793, 80,000 slaves were imported by the French to their sugar islands, and 45 percent of these came from Madagascar. The traditional slave markets on Madagascar and the Comoros were strained to the utmost to meet the demand, and inevitably both the French and their agents sought new sources of supply.[17]

In the late seventeenth century the northwest coast of Madagascar was conquered by Sakalava chiefs from further south. They became the overlords of the Islamic trading communities of the coast, and their power grew through trade with Europeans and the consequent access to supplies of firearms. Throughout the eighteenth century a series of wars between the Sakalava and the Merina kingdom of the plateau helped to keep the slave trade supplied, but toward the end of the century the disputes subsided and the kings of the coast had to seek other sources of slaves. At the same time control of the old pirate coast of northeast Madagascar from Antongil Bay to Tamatave passed into the hands of the Zana Malata, who, led by a half-caste son of the pirate Thomas Tew, set up the kingdom of the Betsimisaraka. The kingdom was short-lived as a single unit, but the Zana Malata chiefs soon became involved in a form of sea-borne piracy far more lucrative than any practiced by their buccaneer ancestors.

The increasing demand for slaves, peace between Merina and Sakalava, and the rise of the predatory Zana Malata chiefs were ingredients for an explosive mixture. Maritime expeditions soon began to be launched to raid the islands and coasts of the Mozambique Channel for slaves.[18] Although contemporaries usually referred to the raiders as Sakalava, their leaders were in fact Betsimisaraka. When an expedition was decided on, the various coastal chiefs of northern Madagascar were informed. The expeditions were then assembled, first on the east coast, and gradually proceeded around the northern end of the island, picking up recruits on the way. The boats were large outrigger canoes, measuring from 7 to 10 meters (23 to 33 feet) long and strengthened with boarding for the ocean crossing. They could carry up to thirty men, and they sailed in massive fleets that sometimes may have consisted of as many as 500 vessels. The final departure took place from Nossi Bé or Majunga, and the first objective was the Comoro Islands.

It now seems clear that the first raids took place around 1795 and were a response to requests by the ruling Almadua clan of Domoni on Anjouan, which wanted aid against its rival, the Almassella of Mutsammudu. Other islands were raided later. The ruler of Mohéli asked for aid against attacks from Anjouan. Mohéli proved an easy target, and the sea-raiders were probably responsible for the destruction of old Niouma Choa, the jungle-grown ruins of which crown a hill a little way from the modern town. Mayotte was also attacked, and Chingoni destroyed; the ruling family took refuge on the tiny islet of Dzaoudzi, which thus began its career as the fortress capital of the island.

The first attack on Grande Comore came in 1798 when the raiders landed in the south at Fumboni. After the attack, the larger towns hastily fortified themselves: Fumboni built a wall and a citadel; Iconi constructed ramparts along the rim of the precipitous volcano that rose above the town; Moroni, Mitsamiouli, Tchudini, and N'tsaoueni all built walls and towers; and Itsandra constructed a citadel linked to the town by a quarter of a mile of walled-in roadway. When the raiders returned in 1802, the population took refuge within the town walls or fled to the hills. The third major attack took place in 1808, and there were further raids in 1810 and 1814. During these years attacks were also made on the East African coast from Kilwa to as far south as central Mozambique, and ships in the Mozambique Channel were stopped and plundered.

To the very real devastation brought by the raids, the sultans of the Comoros responded by seeking assistance from their European associates. Embassies, seeking aid and protection and offering to cede sovereignty, were sent to Bombay, to the Cape of Good Hope, to Mozambique, and to Ile de France.[19] For the most part the embassies returned only with gifts of arms, but one embassy that was sent in

N'tsaoueni (Grande Comore): The town walls facing the sea

1814 to Mauritius (Ile de France was renamed after falling to the British in 1811) did lead to the diplomatic initiative that eventually put an end to the raids. In 1817 Governor Farquhar made an agreement with the Merina king in Madagascar concerning the protection of trade and the end of the slave trade and slave-raiding expeditions. The Merina were now once again at war with the Sakalava chiefs, and the latter increasingly sought the aid of France. Thus, the internal struggle for the control of Madagascar became, in part, a projection of Anglo-French rivalry. By 1820 the Merina had conquered the Sakalava coast, and the raids had ceased; but the event that actually marked the end of the pirate voyages was probably the major defeat suffered by the raiders at the hands of the Portuguese in the Querimba Islands in 1816.

There was Malagasy intervention also in Mayotte. One faction of the feuding ruling families asked their relatives in Madagascar to intervene. The invitation went to the Sakalava chief Andriansouli, whose

Although events in Madagascar eventually put an end to the raids, Malagasy interference in the affairs of the islands was to continue for the next twenty years. The raids had damaged the commerce of the islands and had effected a decline in their population, but they had done nothing to halt the feuds of the ruling clans. On Anjouan the rivalry between Mutsammudu and Domoni led to the sultan inviting a Merina chief, Ramanataka, to settle on the island in 1828. Ramanataka, the general who had conquered the Sakalava coast for the Merina, feared that the new queen, Ranavalona, would seek his life, and he was ready to move with 200 of his followers. Abdullah, the sultan of Anjouan, employed him in the conquest of Mohéli, where, after Abdullah's death, he settled, establishing a Merina chieftaincy on the island.[20]

There was Malagasy intervention also in Mayotte. One faction of the feuding ruling families asked their relatives in Madagascar to intervene. The invitation went to the Sakalava chief Andriansouli, whose position had become very precarious after the Merina conquest. At first Andriansouli merely sent soldiers to support his protégé, but in 1832 he himself moved to Mayotte and settled—inevitably with his military backing becoming the dominant figure on the island. The rivalry between the two Malagasy chiefs, one Merina and the other Sakalava, now resulted in desultory warfare, which affected all four of the islands and prompted the sultan of Anjouan to invite further intervention, this time by the Betsimisaraka chief, Andrianavi, who invaded Mayotte in 1840.[21]

The wars of the Merina and the Sakalava had involved the British and the French in the rivalries of Madagascar. Now these rivalries were extended to the Comoro Islands, and it was only too probable that the archipelago would once again be dragged into the competitive world of the maritime powers. To complicate matters further the Omani sultans of Zanzibar also began to take an interest in the islands. The Zanzibaris presided over a very prosperous East African trading empire and were gradually extending a form of political protection over all the Islamic peoples of the coast. The red flag of the sultanate proved a very important diplomatic badge for traders and slavers of all kinds, and it was to be flown all along the African coast and deep into the interior, in areas where no Zanzibari soldier or official had ever set foot. Allegiance to the Zanzibar sultan came to be seen as an attractive alternative to Malagasy or European domination, and many members of the old ruling clans of the Comoros already had trading connections and family ties with East Africa. Zanzibar itself, however, was also fast becoming an object of Anglo-French rivalry.

THE DEVELOPMENT OF ANGLO-FRENCH RIVALRY

European rivalries in the east seemed to have been brought to an end by British victories in the Napoleonic Wars. Ile de France was captured by the British in 1811 and was retained at the peace; the Dutch lost the Cape of Good Hope and Ceylon. After the peace the British Indian authorities began to extend their informal empire in the Gulf, taking the sultanate of Oman under their wing and encouraging it to extend its influence on the coast of East Africa. Anti-slave trade treaties were gradually forced on the coastal rulers, and as in west Africa, these were designed to open up new regions to British and British Indian commerce. Britain also began to seek faster communications between Europe and India, experimenting with steamers in the Gulf and Red Sea and annexing Aden as a coaling station in 1832. The development of these new routes with their attendant bases deprived the Comoros of a great deal of their importance for international shipping. However, they continued to be used by the squadrons operating against slavers along the coast of eastern Africa.[22]

If the islands no longer seemed crucial to the British commercial empire, they began to feature more prominently in the plans of the

French. France was unwilling to accept its defeat in the Indian Ocean. France retained the island of Réunion, but it lacked a harbor and was unsatisfactory as a base for naval operations. Moreover, because French planters continued to need a large work force, French interest in the Mozambique Channel area increased. Initially the prize was Zanzibar and its trade, the French making a strong bid to dominate the politics of the sultanate by siding with the faction that supported the slave trade. The French also extended their interests in Mozambique and Madagascar in search of commercial outlets and political allies. None of this was likely to alter the balance of power in the Indian Ocean, however, as long as Britain controlled the lines of communication and possessed the naval bases.

It was the search for a naval base that led the French to occupy Nossi Bé in 1838 and to send expeditions to investigate the Comoros in 1840. The open roadsteads and precipitous shores of Grande Comore and Anjouan were clearly of no value, nor was Mohéli's west coast, which was studded with islands. Mayotte, however, was tempting. The French commander, Passot, reported that Mayotte's reef would provide a safe anchorage for a whole fleet. The narrow entrance could be defended, the island was fertile and healthy and could be turned into the "Gibraltar" of the Indian Ocean. In 1841 Passot obtained from Andriansouli, the defacto ruler of Mayotte, a treaty ceding the island to France, and the French government, having ratified the treaty in 1843, began to build their "Gibraltar" on Dzaoudzi.[23]

The immediate result of the French action was to revive active British concern about the Comoros and to give an added twist to the spiral of competition. In 1842 the British forced on Portugal a treaty allowing for the unilateral seizure of suspected slavers; in 1845 a consulate was set up at Zanzibar; and in 1846 the decision was made to set one up on Anjouan as well.[24] On Anjouan the consul was to watch the activities of the French in Mayotte and to reestablish the informal British protectorate over the island. The consul was also responsible for implementing a treaty outlawing the slave trade made with the sultan of Anjouan in 1844. The Anjouan consulate was the cheapest and most effective counter to the French that Britain could devise. It drew Anjouan firmly into Britain's informal empire and prevented further French annexations. In 1854 a British consulate was established in Mozambique, and in 1856, to crown this extension of British influence, the British protégé, Said Majid, was securely installed on the throne of Zanzibar.

During the 1850s the French made no further moves in the region of the Comoros. The turmoil that had accompanied the 1848 revolutions in Europe had given way to a period when the French were anxious to remain on good terms with the British. Moreover, Mayotte had been found to be rather less than a new "Gibraltar." French settlers and servicemen died in large numbers through disease, and the dangers of the reef, so thoroughly understood in earlier times by the captains of

119,487   LIBRARY
College of St. Francis
JOLIET, ILLINOIS

sailing vessels, were now perceived to outweigh the security provided by the lagoon.[25] Furthermore, all supplies had to be brought into the base, and after 1850 further work on its fortification ceased. The two powers were content to share influence; the French continued to dominate Mayotte, and the British Anjouan. Grande Comore, independent of overt European pressure, became increasingly subject to the attentions of the sultan of Zanzibar, and the fact that a Malagasy dynasty continued to occupy the throne of Mohéli left that island exposed to foreign influence also. Although there was some political stability during this era, economic changes were about to transform the islands. For at least five centuries the ruling clans of the Comoros had made their living by trading with visiting ships or by acting as clearing agents for the slave trade. Their prosperity depended on the strategic position of their towns on the major sea-lanes from Kilwa to Madagascar and from Europe to India. In the nineteenth century this age-old commerce began to wither. The pirate raids of the Betsimisaraka stripped the islands of wealth and population; British cruisers drove the slave trade underground and made it virtually impossible after 1844 for the trade to continue in any but the most clandestine manner. Then, in 1869 the Suez Canal was opened, and the main shipping lanes of the Indian Ocean were diverted by way of Egypt. Fewer and fewer ships visited the islands. Between 1852 and 1858 an average of forty-six foreign ships a year stopped for provisions at Anjouan, half of them American whalers. In 1864–1865 only three ships stopped. The disappearance of the whalers was a result of the American Civil War (in 1864 one of the visitors had been the famous Southern commerce raider, the *Alabama*), but British ships also ceased to call after about 1855.[26]

As the old commerce died, new economic activity was coming to life. Mauritius and Réunion were enjoying prosperity as sugar islands, and the planters and their financiers were eager to open new fields of production. The Comoros, with their long-established reputation for fertility and their considerable tracts of virgin land, became objects of great interest.

The first plantations were probably started on Anjouan by Ramanataka, the fugitive Merina general, who began to develop the fertile land around Pomoni. After 1843 French sugar planters moved into Mayotte, and in 1850 the British consul in Anjouan, William Sunley, started his successful sugar factory by taking over the estates at Pomoni. Arab landowners soon began to take an interest in these foreign enterprises. In Anjouan the sultan himself set up a large sugar plantation at Bambao near the old town of Domoni. In both Grande Comore and Mohéli concessions were granted to foreign adventurers, and in each case the ruler became, to a limited extent, a partner in the enterprise.

Although William Sunley was the leading sugar planter in the islands until his death in 1877, the decline of maritime trade and the rise of the plantations signaled the decline of British and the rise of

French influence. This process can best be examined by looking at each of the islands in turn.

THE FRENCH IN MAYOTTE

When France annexed Mayotte in 1843, the island was in the hands of the Sakalava followers of Andriansouli, but there was also a remnant of the old Arab ruling class, which had been partly dispossessed. The sultan of Anjouan claimed sovereignty over the island and repeatedly sent Malagasy mercenaries to harry the island. As a result Mayotte was largely depopulated. The French estimated that, slaves apart, the population numbered only 1,800 in 1843 and about 5,600 in 1846, when the refugees had begun to return.[27]

The cession of the island to the French by Andriansouli was widely disputed by those who claimed he had possessed no sovereign rights in the first place. The sultan of Anjouan continued to maintain that he was the rightful ruler and appealed to Britain for help. The Sakalava chiefs also claimed that the cession was not binding. They resisted the establishment of a French administration, and when Andriansouli died in 1845, tried to elect his son, Bangala, ruler in his place. The French refused to recognize Bangala and had to face revolts by the chiefs in 1849, 1854, and 1856; these revolts increasingly took on the aspect of popular movements as the chiefs were joined by the plantation workers and maroons.[28]

The French administration threatened the economic position of the chiefs as well as ending their political independence. In 1847 the French abolished slavery on the island, and half of the 2,730 slaves left the island with their masters, the rest being set free with compensation paid.[29] The land of Mayotte was then divided into concessions, two-thirds of which were allotted to French planters from Réunion. In this way the traditional ruling class was largely dispossessed, and feudal, social, and economic relations gave way to those of plantation capitalism.

Although French interest in Mayotte as a Naval base waned in the 1850s, the government never seriously considered abandoning the island and toyed with a number of different projects for extracting value from their colony. A free port to rival the commercial supremacy of Zanzibar was suggested, as was a penal colony. These ideas, however, were abandoned, and the authorities were left with no alternative but to encourage the creole planters. These gradually took up their concessions, cutting the forest to make cane fields and expelling the native Mahorais into the hills. Production of sugar grew impressively at first, and the authorities found themselves under pressure to provide the needed labor. They turned to Mozambique, where the slave trade still continued more or less openly, and they intervened in the affairs of the other islands with the idea of securing supplies of contract laborers from them as well. By the 1870s there were some 3,340 *engagé* laborers at work. The arrival of these African immigrants stimulated a rapid growth in the population, the census of 1855 recording a total of 11,540. Few of these ever returned to Africa, but a number did escape from the plantations and formed a maroon community in the hills, which helped to make Mayotte extremely lawless. Because of this lawlessness and the prevalence of disease, the planters lived, for the most part, under the protection of the garrison, crossing to Dzaoudzi at night or living on board ship.

In 1890, 4,235 tonnes (4,168 tons) of sugar were being produced annually by the eighteen factories on Mayotte, but the industry was in decline as prices slumped and bad harvests affected yields.[30] One after another the plantations went out of business, the cane fields were overgrown by bush, and the creole families were reduced to poverty. Mayotte, however, remained the center of French politics in the region. An official hospital, barracks, and school were set up, and justice was carried out by a mixed tribunal. All this official activity, however, was carried on from the tiny islet of Dzaoudzi or from nearby Pamanzi, with which it was connected by a causeway, and the rest of Mayotte was little affected. Nevertheless, the island carried with it into the twentieth century many influences deriving from the French settlement. The population remained strongly Malagasy in many of its cultural traits, from the local language and the type of house construction to the low level of Islamic influence, but French rule accounted for the relatively significant number of Christians among the population, particularly among the descendants of the plantation workers, and the importance of the creoles in the island's affairs. This dominance of Malagasy and French influence formed the origin of Mayotte separatism, which became such a problem in the second half of the twentieth century.

MOHÉLI

After 1832 the island of Mohéli had passed ever more firmly under the control of Ramanataka and his Merina followers, who numbered 600 in all, and who formed a powerful faction among the island's population. Nevertheless, for four or five years he had to maneuver carefully in the world of Comorian politics—there were threats from Anjouan and from the Sakalava of Mayotte, and Ramanataka himself dabbled in the politics of Grande Comore. To make his position more secure he adopted Islam, changed his name to Abderrahman, and consented to fly the flag of Zanzibar. However, before his death in 1841, he switched his allegiance to France and left instructions to his heir to depend solely on French friendship.[31]

Ramanataka's heir was a seven-year-old girl who at once became the victim of the rival factions of the Merina and the Arabs, the former generally favoring France and the latter Zanzibar. The French initially tried to maintain their influence by appointing a governess for the queen and arranging for her coronation, but in 1851 a coup inspired in Zanzibar brought an eligible Arab prince from Zanzibar who married the young queen and raised the red flag of the sultanate. Zanzibar maintained a virtual protectorate throughout the 1850s, the period when French influence generally declined in the western Indian Ocean, and the British established an ascendancy in Zanzibar itself. Then, in the 1860s the penetration of plantation capital, already far advanced in Mayotte and Anjouan, began to affect Mohéli as well.

Pro-French, Merina elements expelled the Zanzibaris in 1860, and power in the palace passed to a young French adventurer, Joseph François Lambert, who had made a name for himself in Madagascan politics. Lambert obtained from the queen a concession (eventually signed in February 1865) that was worded in such a way that he could claim possession of the whole of the island. Article 1 bestowed on him *"toutes les terres qu'il voudra prendre pour mettre en valeur l'île de Mohéli."* The queen became a partner in the enterprise, receiving 5 percent of all profits. Lambert began to develop his concession with capital from Réunion.[32] He also helped the Mayotte planters recruit contract labor in Mohéli, and in his turn was supported by periodic visits from French warships. Lambert's ascendancy in the island was not uneventful, however. In 1867, during Lambert's absence, islanders favorable to Zanzibar plundered his house and raised the flag of the sultanate, and an attempt was made to undo his concession by persuading the queen to abdicate in favor of her son.[33] However, Lambert was brought back by French warships, and his concession was confirmed, so that after 1871 the influence of France and French concessionaires was stronger than ever. Lambert died in 1873, and in 1881 his concession was taken over by the Sunley interests from Anjouan. In 1886 France imposed a formal protectorate treaty when it seemed that there was a serious possibility of the Germans making a bid to control the Comoros.

The period of the protectorate lasted until the formal annexation in 1912. The sultanate, through which the French resident first tried to rule, rapidly lost any prestige it still retained and ended, in practice, when the last queen eloped with a French gendarme in 1901 and went to live on a farm in the south of France. Power lay formally with the French resident, but belonged, in reality, to those who held Lambert's concession. The labor demands of the concessionaires and the grievances of the Mohélians who had lost their land made the period of the protectorate one of chronic lawlessness marked by frequent outbreaks of social unrest.

Mohéli remained the poorest and most neglected of the islands, the decline of the Merina ruling class and the dominance of the French concessionaires leaving it without an effective indigenous class of notables. Excluded from any say in the affairs of the archipelago under the French, and after 1975 under the independent government of Moroni, the Mohélians retained something of a tradition of popular dissidence,

Entrance to a public square in Moroni

which came strongly to the fore in their defiance of Ali Soilih's government in 1978.

GRANDE COMORE

The nineteenth century witnessed a long drawn-out struggle for the control of Grande Comore between the two sultanates of Itsandra and Bambao, a struggle that predictably involved the intervention of outsiders. These two diminutive states lay next to one another on the western side of the island. Bambao was made up of the two towns of Iconi and Moroni, the latter having a passable harbor for small boats. Barely three miles to the north lay Itsandra, beautifully situated on one arm of a wide sandy bay. Two miles inland, and considerably above sea level, was the large town of Tjudini. Each of these four towns was only half an hour's walk from its nearest neighbor, and their constantly feuding families must have been uncomfortably close to one another. The events of the century, with their tangle of marriage alliances and personal feuds, were chronicled by one of the participants, Said Bakari, so that, for once, a wholly Comorian perspective on events is possible.[34]

There were twelve sultanates on Grande Comore, nominally independent of one another but recognizing a *primus inter pares* who took the title of "Sultan Thibé." Much of the feuding between the ruling clans was ostensibly over the right to use this title. Although largely honorific, its possession gave the holder some right to mediate in island disputes and could be represented to foreigners as conferring sovereignty over the island as a whole.

In the early part of the nineteenth century the Malagasy raids had led the sultan of Bambao to appeal for aid to outsiders. He made an unsuccessful attempt to hand the island over to the Portuguese in return for assistance and eventually succeeded in obtaining some firearms from the British. In the longer term these activities served only to intensify the island's feuds. Once the raids were over, both Bambao and Itsandra sought allies abroad, the former in Anjouan and Mayotte, the latter among the Merina in Mohéli. The French commandant of Mayotte visited Grande Comore in 1843 and concluded agreements for the recruitment of contract laborers and the right to cut timber. He set up a sawmill on the island and tried to look after the interests of his protégé, Said Achmet, in Moroni. Instead of strengthening the position of Bambao, however, French support weakened and undermined the sultanate. Said Achmet became increasingly isolated on the island, even among his own former supporters. In 1865 his authority could only be maintained by the visit of a French gunboat.[35]

Nevertheless, when Said Achmet eventually died in 1875, the French hastened to confirm their influence in the island by recognizing as Sultan Thibé and as ruler of Bambao, Said Ali, a man who had received a French education in Mayotte. Said Ali had to establish himself in the face of widespread opposition from the Arab families who received active help from Zanzibar, where one of their number acted as the chief of police.

By 1883 Said Ali had fought his way to power in the island, his principal rival being allowed to die of starvation in prison. However, his position was precarious, and France's interests would have been far from secure but for the arrival that year of a naturalist, Léon Humblot, who had just been on a scientific expedition to Madagascar. Humblot set about examining the flora and fauna of the island and was the first person to name a number of new species. At the same time he showed talent as an entrepreneur, and following the example of Lambert on Mohéli, obtained from Said Ali a concession that, in effect, made him the virtual owner of the island. Said Ali agreed to concede to him any land he wished to cultivate and to supply him with the requisite contract labor in return for 10 percent of the profits.[36] Said Ali feared Italian and German infiltration and may have hoped to buy French protection by ceding land that he knew was not really his to give away. Humblot believed, rightly as it proved, that in the frantic atmosphere of the scramble for Africa, the important thing was to be in possession, without paying too much attention to the soundness of any title.

The enormity of Humblot's concession had the immediate effect of stimulating opposition to Said Ali. The sultan of Badjini in the south of the island contacted the Zanzibaris and also approached the Germans, who in 1884–1885 were busy establishing points of influence on the African coast. A German agent, Karl Schmidt, arrived with a flag, which was flown from the citadel of Fumboni. This rash and desperate measure brought rapid and direct French intervention. A warship shelled Fumboni, and the German flag was unceremoniously pulled down. A French protectorate over the whole of the island was then declared and a resident installed.

The declaration of the protectorate did nothing to calm the situation on the island. Opposition to the French, to Said Ali, and to Humblot increased. French marines had to be landed to hunt down the former sultan of Badjini in the forests. In 1890 Said Ali was so unpopular that he was forced to flee the island; he was brought back ignominiously in a French gunboat and was still more ignominiously awarded the *légion d'honneur*. In 1893 he fled again, accused of being involved in an abortive attempt to murder Humblot. This time he was not brought back and remained in exile in Réunion. The island passed under the total control of Humblot, who was appointed resident by the French.

From 1892 to 1896 Humblot ruled Grande Comore as a despot. He was director of the Société de Grande Comore (SAGC), which was incorporated on the basis of his concession; he was the resident and acted as judge of the mixed courts. He armed his own militia, lent money to the islanders, and foreclosed when they failed to pay, hearing the cases in his own court. The children of the islanders found themselves "apprenticed" to Humblot's plantations, where the workers were paid with chits to be cashed at Humblot's stores.

In 1896 the French authorities were roused to action by the scandal of Humblot's seignorial rule. He was replaced as resident, and in 1897 a ministerial decree settled relations between the SAGC and the island's government. This decree included a land settlement that recognized the rights of Comorians in the land that they farmed. Humblot easily evaded such attempts to restrain him. He saw thirteen residents come and go between 1896 and 1904 and continued to maintain his own force of company police. The land settlement was carried out by an officer nominated by Humblot who allotted 47 percent of the land of the island to the SAGC. Finally, Humblot negotiated a remission of taxation for the company for the next fifty years. His position remained unchallenged until his death in 1914, and his heirs continued litigation until 1927 in order to obtain the maximum amount of land.

The French found it equally difficult to deal with Said Ali, the other partner of the original concession. Although in exile, the sultan had never abdicated and continued to hold extensive rights as party to the agreement. He refused to make any settlement with the French until he was cleared of any involvement in the alleged assassination attempt on Humblot. The litigation over the rights of Said Ali became something of a *cause célèbre* for French politicians, who seemed to yearn for another Dreyfus case. It was only in 1910 that Said Ali was finally exonerated and agreed to sign an abdication paper than enabled the French government to finalize the merger of the island with Madagascar in 1914.[37]

This helplessness of a government in the face of a company that had obtained a concession and could sue for damages if any attempt was made to alter its terms is one of the features of the extension of European power in the world. On the tiny stage of Grande Comore it led to the creation of a semi-feudal despotism, comparable perhaps only to the corporate feudalism of the concessionaires in Portuguese Mozambique and equally difficult to control. Although the extent of the SAGC concession was modified somewhat in 1927, it was not until after World War II that the then owner of the company was forced to disgorge significant amounts of land and to subordinate the company to the colonial administration.

ANJOUAN

Anjouan had always been the richest and most densely populated of the Comoro Islands, and the pretensions of its sultans had often been decisive in the affairs of the archipelago. The French occupation of Mayotte in 1843 made the sultans fear the imminent fall of their own island to the French, and the successive interventions of the French in Mohéli and Grande Comore seemed to suggest that that was likely to happen.

The only practical alternative was to establish firmer ties with the British. In 1844 Sultan Salim signed a treaty with Britain outlawing the slave trade, and in 1848 he allowed the British to establish a consulate on Anjouan. This was not only a political move designed to check French influence and confirm the power of the Mutsammudu ruling clan, it was also a move toward the introduction of plantation agriculture. Salim had actively sought European capital and had eventually let a concession to two partners, Josiah Napier and William Sunley. It was Napier who became the first British consul, and following his death, the post passed to Sunley. Until he died in 1877, Sunley was to be the dominant influence on Anjouan, and he single-handedly maintained an informal empire for Britain on the island. At Pomoni he developed sugar plantations and introduced refining machinery that produced one and a half tons of sugar a day, making him far more successful than any of his French counterparts on Mayotte. He also created the harbor at Pomoni by blasting the rocks, and he set up a small coaling depot for British ships. Abdallah, who succeeded Salim as sultan in 1855, was a friend and admirer of Sunley. Under his influence sugar estates were developed near the old town of Domoni, capital being raised in Mauritius and the requisite machinery imported.

Plantation agriculture brought social and, in the end, political change to Anjouan. To supply his plantation with labor, Sunley had approached the Arab slave owners on the island and had hired their slaves from them. Although Sunley paid his laborers a wage, it soon became known that the Arab owners took three-fifths of the pay and that the workers were little better off than slaves. The news reached the Foreign Office in London, and in 1865 Sunley was forced to resign as consul. Britain made no further appointment, but Sunley's continued presence in the island and the expansion of his business meant that British influence was still dominant. Sunley was more successful at producing sugar than the French planters, and on Lambert's death he took over the Mohéli concessions, thereby threatening to absorb that island into his personal empire.[38]

Sultan Abdallah's plantations were, on the other hand, less successful. He ran into debt, and the first of his sugar reached the market just as sugar prices were falling. However, at Bambao he assembled a work force brought in from Mozambique, and he armed his slaves to form a sort of private army. He built himself a palace away from his capital city and increasingly resided there. The Arab notables became more and more alienated and hostile to his rule.

In 1882 Britain cajoled the sultan into signing a treaty for the abolition of all slavery on Anjouan. This move was intensely unpopular among the Arab ruling class and, had Abdallah implemented it, would have proved politically disastrous. Being deeply in debt to Mauritius bankers, the sultan sought a way out of his many difficulties by appealing to the French for protection. In 1886 the French offered him a protection treaty that limited his freedom to conduct foreign affairs and secured the succession. Abdallah accepted, but the following year the French demanded the right to appoint a resident and began to interfere in the island's internal affairs. Abdallah signed a new treaty in October 1887 after having been persuaded of the wisdom of doing so by the arrival of a French gunboat. Two years later the French forced their own anti-slavery agreement on the sultan in order to head off any further British interference. However, this treaty, instead of freeing the slaves outright, made provision for five years of contract labor to follow enfranchisement. Slave unrest arose immediately and was fanned by many members of the old Arab ruling class, who resented the loss of their independence to France. The rebels found a leader in Said Othman, and they installed him as sultan in Mutsammudu.[39]

As the scale of the revolt became apparent, the French mustered their forces to intervene. An aged Arab notable, Said Omar, who was the father of Said Ali—the French puppet sultan of Grande Comore—was declared ruler, and a strong force aboard three warships appeared off Mutsammudu, which duly surrendered. The French then turned their attention to suppressing the jacquerie in the countryside. The coastal regions were exposed to attack from the sea, and the rebels retreated inland, where the final battles with the French took place in June 1889. The revolt had involved some 2,500 former slaves and was the most serious revolt of its kind that the French had to face in the Comoros. Although the uprising was suppressed, the slaves did achieve their main objective: slavery was abolished forthwith without any period of contractual labor.[40]

The new French resident was generous with the distribution of land concessions. The former sultan's estates at Bambao went to French concessionaires, who consolidated their holdings into the Société de Bambao in 1907. A puppet sultan continued to occupy the throne but without any power. He was eventually persuaded to abdicate in 1909 after an American plantation owner, Wilson, successfully challenged the legal powers of the French resident. The irregularities of the French position in the island and a general desire to tighten up colonial administration led to demands for a more formal arrangement, and following the abdication, Anjouan was incorporated along with the other islands in the colony of Madagascar in 1914.

The ruling Arab elites on Anjouan survived better than their counterparts on the other islands because they had not succumbed to Malagasy dominance in the early 1800s and had preserved their social position and much of their land during the years of the protectorate. They were to be a formidably powerful group once politics became a possible pursuit for Comorians after World War II.

THE NINETEENTH CENTURY IN RETROSPECT

Studied in isolation from the rest of the world, the events of the Comoro Islands in the nineteenth century—marked by clan rivalry and the rapid passage of shadowy queens and sultans across the political stage—appear confusing and incoherent. However, the Comorians did not exist in isolation; they were affected by and played their part in the political and economic forces in the world at large. The rise of the slave trade in the western Indian Ocean in the eighteenth century had been both an opportunity and a disaster. The Comorian market in slaves had continued virtually without interruption until 1844 when Britain imposed on Anjouan a treaty banning the trade. Many Arab families had enjoyed considerable prosperity as a result of slaving and had formed commercial ties with Madagascar, Mozambique, and Zanzibar. However, the slave trade had also instigated the raids of the pirates, which had resulted in severe depopulation and destruction of the islands' agriculture.

Initially the French intervention was a strategic move, an attempt to establish a naval base from which to rebuild French power in the Indian Ocean, a move that Britain countered by appointing a consul with a watching brief to Anjouan. Very soon it became apparent that this renewal of interest in the islands by the French and British was the harbinger of major change in the region's economy. No longer were European vessels merely calling for refreshment en route to the East; in fact the number of foreign ships calling at the islands began to decline noticeably, and plantation capital from Réunion and Mauritius began to seek investment opportunities in the islands. The concession hunters found the warring chiefs easy prey. The rulers who made the concessions also stood to gain, either politically through foreign support or economically through the receipt of dividends or by developing plantations on their own estates.

As with concessions granted elsewhere in Africa, scant regard was paid to whether the concession was legal or whether the chief had the right to make the concession (it was certain, for example, that Said Ali had no right to cede land in the territory of the other rulers of Grande Comore). Nor was any concern expressed that the islanders dispossessed by the concessions should receive compensation. The concessionaires, however outrageous their claims, could generally expect French diplomatic and even military support, and this official backing was used to extort from the island rulers the labor needed to develop the concessions.[41] Recruiting rights formed part of the political deals made with the island rulers, and contract laborers were introduced from Mozambique so that the growth of the islands' population during the century was largely due to the arrival of this new servile class. A final aspect of the capitalist revolution was the alienation of timber-cutting rights. Early on the French began to exploit the timber on Grande Comore, and timber rights were part of the restructured Lambert concession in 1871.

To this invasion of foreign capital the ruling families had little resistance to offer. They tried to resume control of affairs by forcing abdication of the responsible sultans, and they tried to use the influence of Zanzibar as a counterweight, but repeatedly the French showed their willingness to enforce contracts with gunboats and to maintain the Francophile rulers in power. This French dominance through client-rulers and French companies had already set a pattern that France was to resume after the formal dismantling of its empire in the 1960s. It was neo-colonialism before colonialism had even arrived.

By the mid-1880s, however, this policy had become ineffective. The client-rulers had lost their local following, and indirect rule became increasingly difficult to operate. Moreover, the increasing pace of the scramble for Africa made the risk of sudden intervention from Britain or Germany very real. In 1884 Germany declared its protectorate on the East African coast, forcing Britain to formalize its protectorate over Zanzibar and eventually to take action to secure a sector of East Africa for itself. The long-standing British influence on Anjouan and the presence of British missionaries in Madagascar suggested that Britain might seek to formalize these relations as well. Fearing such a move, particularly after Britain had imposed a treaty banning slavery on Anjouan in 1882, France moved to negotiate formal protectorates and to impose French residents. As with so many other similar moves at the time of the scramble for Africa, France's motives were largely preemptive—to prevent any of its rivals from occupying the islands.

In the case of each of the Comoro Islands, France's move was vigorously but ineffectually opposed by the Arab ruling class, which was often in temporary alliance with the servile population. It was another twenty-five years before France set up any kind of colonial administration, and the intervening years were a period dominated by the concession companies cultivating export crops for world markets.

While the Arab ruling class saw its political power pass into the hands of the French-backed sultans and foreign concessionaires, the peasant population of the islands experienced partial expropriation, losing much of their best agricultural land. Driven into the mountains, they increasingly found an identity of interest with the newly arrived contract laborers and with the class of former slaves. Revolts occurred in all four islands, and temporary, if somewhat unnatural, alliances were achieved between the politically dispossessed chiefs and the economically dispossessed peasants and former laborers.

The defeat of this opposition by the French was inevitable since the islanders had no weapons with which to oppose the gunboats and machine guns of the French. However, their defeat was equally the result of the economic power and technological superiority of the concessionaires and the fact that the alternative economy, which had depended on maritime trade and the supply of visiting ships, had dwindled almost to the vanishing point.

Street in the old part
of Moroni

COLONIAL ADMINISTRATION

When Mayotte was first ceded to France in 1841, it became the
responsibility of the governor of Réunion. In 1843, however, the annexation of the island was ratified in France, and it was made a
dependency of Nossi Bé. These were the days when France was actively
promoting the idea of a "Gibraltar" in the Indian Ocean, and so in
1845 the headquarters of their operations in this area was moved to
Mayotte, and the commandant there was made responsible for Nossi
Bé, Nossi Comba, and Sainte Marie as well. These three islands were
detached from Mayotte in 1853 and became separate commands. Mayotte

was then governed as an individual colony until 1899. Meanwhile in 1886, the other three Comoro islands became French protectorates, directly the responsibility of the minister of Marine and the Colonies. In 1899 the governor of Mayotte assumed responsibility for the protectorates, and in this year, for the first time in their history, all four islands came nominally under a single political authority.[42]

While the French had been consolidating their position in the Comoros, they had been acquiring nearby Madagascar. Germany and Britain had waived all claims, and General Galliéni had arrived to pacify the island and to replace the Merina sovereignty with that of France. In 1897 the last queen of Madagascar was exiled, and royalty was abolished. However, if France had been prepared to spend lavishly on the military conquests, it was less willing to spend money on turning its soldiers' swords into ploughshares. In 1900 the French assembly required that all the colonies in their hastily scrambled together empire should be self-sufficient and should pay their way. Galliéni gave way to Victor Augagneur, and a program of administrative economies and tidy bureaucratic methods was established in Madagascar. It seemed wholly logical that the four tiny Comoro Islands should form part of the colony of Madagascar and should not be expected to support a separate establishment. Mayotte and the three protectorates were joined to Madagascar by a decree on April 9, 1908. The survival of sultanates in the protectorates now appeared an embarrassing anomaly. One by one the sultans were forced to abdicate; the sultan of Anjouan in 1909; Said Ali of Grand Comore in 1910, after long litigation; and the last ruler of Mohéli, in 1912. It was in 1912, therefore, that the four islands assumed the same colonial status, and in 1914 the last vestiges of their separate status disappeared when they became part of Madagascar. Dzaoudzi became a simple center of a civil circumscription.[43]

It is widely acknowledged that the thirty-two years during which the Comoros were fully part of Madagascar were years of stagnation and neglect, with the land concession companies being the real rulers of the islands. Comorians were taught to look to Madagascar for employment, for education, and even for basic health facilities, and the number of Comorians who went to Majunga, Diego Suarez, and other towns in Madagascar grew steadily during the 1920s and 1930s.

Although technically they formed part of a single state, the Comoro Islands and Madagascar were never successfully integrated. The Comorian population retained its distinctive identity, and even families that had been resident at Majunga for generations considered themselves Comorian rather than Malagasy. The Comorian population formed the most vigorous and the largest section of Madagascar's Muslim population, and the communal differences between them and the Malagasy were sufficiently clear-cut to be exploited by the French. For instance, the French felt it safe to exile Joseph Ravoahangy, an early leader of Malagasy nationalism, to the Comoros in 1916 and to recruit Comorian police for work in the

large Madagascar towns. In 1946 Comorian police and Malagasy servicemen were involved in communal riots in Tananarive, and in 1947,
when a widespread revolt broke out in Madagascar, the authorities once
again recruited Comorians into the security forces.[44]

The Comoro Islands did not prosper under the dead hand of
provincial administration. There were no public institutions where the
art of politics could be practiced, and the very limited budget precluded
the development of even a basic infrastructure of communications. The
large companies ruled the lives of Comorians, and although there was
a measure of decentralization in 1925 and some land reform in 1926,
little impression was made on a society dominated by a feudal Arab
landowning class and by equally feudal plantation companies.

With the outbreak of war in 1939, it at first looked as though
Madagascar would side with de Gaulle. However, the Vichy regime sent
out Governor Annet, who was able to induce the colony to accept Vichy
neutrality. It is likely that the war would have passed Madagascar by
but for the fear of Japanese activity in the western Indian Ocean. The
British believed that the great natural harbor of Diego Suarez was at
risk and on May 5, 1942, launched a surprise amphibious attack on the
port. The success of the action at first appeared doubtful, and a Japanese
submarine attacked and damaged one of the British cruisers, but the
port fell, and British and South African troops continued to occupy the
other garrisoned areas of the colony. On July 2, 1942, Mayotte was
taken by a British force, and the Comoros, after a brief occupation,
were restored to the government of Free France.[45]

NOTES

1. R. Kent, "The Possibilities of Indonesian Colonies in Africa with Special
Reference to Madagascar," in C. Mehaud, ed., *Mouvements des populations dans
l'Océan Indien* (Paris: Champion, 1979), pp. 93–105.

2. Pierre Vérin, "Aspects de la civilisation des echelles anciennes du nord
de Madagascar," in C. Mehaud, ed., *Mouvements des populations dans l'Océan
Indien*, pp. 61–90.

3. T. A. Chumovsky, ed., *Tres roteiros desconhecidos de Ahmed Ibn-Majid*
(Lisbon: Commissão Executiva das Comemorações do V Centenário da Morte
do Infante D. Henrique, 1960), pp. 51–52; G. R. Tibbetts, *Arab Navigation in
the Indian Ocean Before the Coming of the Portuguese* (London: Royal Asiatic
Society, 1971), p. 435.

4. Letter of Pedro Ferreira to King Manuel, August 31, 1506, in E. Axelson,
South-East Africa 1488–1530 (London: Longmans, 1940), pp. 240–244.

5. Nevil Chittick, "The 'Shirazi' Colonisation of East Africa," in J. D. Fage
and R. Oliver, eds., *Papers in African Pre-History* (Cambridge: Cambridge
University Press, 1970), pp. 257–276; B. Martin, "Arab Migration to East Africa
in Medieval Times," *African Historical Studies* 8 (1974), pp. 367–389.

6. The traditional histories of the Comoros are potentially a very rich
source for Swahili history and culture. Many of the texts are still in the process
of recovery and publication, but others have been known for some time and

were used, in various forms, by early writers on the Comoros, such as A. L. Gevrey, *Essai sur les Comores* (Pondichery: A. Saligny, 1870) and A. Völtzkow, *Die Comoren,* vol. 1, pt. 1, of *Reise in Ost-Afrika* (Stuttgart: Heckmann Wentzel Stiftung, 1914). To date the most important complete text to have been edited is Gernot Rotter, ed., *Muslimische inseln vor Ostafrika; eine arabische komoren-chronik des 19 jahrhunderts,* Beiruter Texte und Studien, Band 18 (Beirut: Franz Steiner, 1976). Important also is C. Alibert, M. Ahmed Chamanga, and G. Boulinier, *Texte, traduction et interprétation du manuscrit de Chingoni;* première partie, *Asie du sud-est et monde insulindien* 7 (1976), pp. 25–62, and the works cited therein. A list of some of the most important traditional histories with a brief discussion was included as an appendix to M. Newitt, "The Comoro Islands in Indian Ocean Trade Before the Nineteenth Century," the cyclostyled proceedings of Section III of the International Conference on Indian Ocean Studies, Perth, 1979.

7. João de Castro, *Roteiro de Lisboa a Goa,* vol. 1 of A. Cortesão and L. de Albuquerque, eds., *Obras completas de D. João de Castro* (Coimbra: Academia Internacional da Cultura Portuguesa, 1968), p. 247.

8. The trade of the Comoro Islands and their relations with the Portuguese have been discussed in two articles by M. Newitt, "The Southern Swahili Coast in the First Century of European Expansion," *Azania* 13 (1978), pp. 111–126 and "The Comoro Islands in Indian Ocean Trade Before the Nineteenth Century."

9. Grandidier, A. and Grandidier, G., eds., *Collection des Ouvrages Anciens Concernant Madagascar* (hereafter *COACM*), 9 vols. (Paris, 1903–1920), vol. 1, p. 395.

10. Ibid., p. 395; and Edward Monox to East India Company, December 28, 1617, in F. C. Danvers, ed., *Letters Received by the East India Company,* 6 vols. (London: Sampson Low, 1896), vol. 6, p. 271; and Richard Allnutt to East India Company, Surat, January 31, 1634, *Calendar of State Papers: East Indies and Persia 1630–1634* (London: Her Majesty's Stationery Office, 1892), vol. 8, no. 534, p. 517.

11. See, for example, Captain Cornwall, "Observations on Several Voyages to India," in T. Astley, ed., *A New General Collection of Voyages and Travels,* 4 vols. (London: Astley, 1745–1747), vol. 3, p. 392.

12. Urbain Faurec, *L'Archipel des sultans batailleurs* (Tananarive: Imprimerie Nationale, 1941); new edition (Moroni: Promo Al Camar, n.d.), pp. 38–40.

13. Cornwall, "Observations on Several Voyages to India," p. 392.

14. *COACM,* vol. 3, pp. 560–561.

15. Daniel Defoe, *A General History of the Pyrates* (London: Dent, 1972), pp. 118–121; Charles Grey, *Pirates of the Eastern Seas* (London: Sampson Low, 1933).

16. Sir William Jones, "Remarks on the Island of Hinzuan, or Johanna," *Asiatic Researches* (London, 1807), vol. 2, p. 104. Emphasis in original.

17. E. A. Alpers, "The French Slave Trade in East Africa 1721–1810," *Cahiers d'études africaines* 10 (1970), pp. 80–124.

18. For the Sakalava pirate raids see B. Dubins, "A Political History of the Comoro Islands 1795–1886" (Ph.D. diss., Boston, 1975), Chap. 4.

19. One of the most bizarre episodes in the whole history of the islands occurred in 1803 when, in return for a gift of arms, the sultan of Anjouan was persuaded to accept thirty-six French deportees—thirty-three of them ex-Jacobin terrorists involved in a plot against Napoleon. Apart from four who escaped in a boat, all these exiles died within a very short time. See Dubins, "A Political

History of the Comoro Islands," pp. 70–71; and J. Manicacci, "Les derniers terroristes à Anjouan," *Bulletin de l'Académie Malgache* 29 (1950), pp. 14–19.

20. Dubins, "A Political History of the Comoro Islands," pp. 98–102, 168–169.

21. Ibid., pp. 133–139; Thierry Flobert, *Les Comores*, Travaux et mémoires de la faculté de droit et de science politique d'Aix-Marseille No. 24 (Marseille: Aix-Marseilles P.U., 1974), pp. 51–57.

22. The best account of the war, trade, and diplomacy of this period is still G. S. Graham, *Great Britain in the Indian Ocean 1810–1850* (Oxford: Clarendon Press, 1967).

23. Flobert, *Les Comores*, pp. 57–69; also Gevrey, *Essai sur les Comores*, p. 223.

24. The British consul, Josiah Napier, actually took up his office in 1848, and the papers of the Comoro Consulate (which lasted until his successor, William Sunley, resigned in 1865) are contained in the Public Record Office (PRO) FO 19. Other papers on the Comoro Consulate are included in FO 54 (Zanzibar) and FO 84 (Slave Trade).

25. A New England captain visiting Mayotte in 1849 recorded, "While we lay here the average deaths were about 8 frenchmen a day." Quoted in N. R. Bennett and George E. Brooks, *New England Merchants in Africa* (Boston: Boston University Press, 1965), p. 417.

26. PRO FO 19 (5) Sunley to Clarendon, "Report upon the Trade of the Comoro Islands for the Year ending December 31st 1857"; and PRO FO 19 (8) "Report upon the Trade of the Comoro Islands for the Year 1864." Sunley writes in this latter report, "The Alabama visited Johanna and owing probably to the presence of this vessel in these areas, no American whale ships called at the island."

27. Gevrey, *Essai sur les Comores*, p. 251.

28. For French rule in Mayotte see Dubins, "A Political History of the Comoro Islands," Chap. 6; Flobert, *Les Comores*, pp. 57–72; and Gevrey, *Essai sur les Comores*, Chap. 3.

29. Jean Martin, "L'affranchissement des esclaves de Mayotte décembre 1846–juillet 1847," *Cahiers d'études africaines* 16 (1976), pp. 207–233.

30. Flobert, *Les Comores*, p. 263.

31. For events in Mohéli see Gevrey, *Essai sur les Comores*, pp. 139–169, and Dubins, "A Political History of the Comoro Islands," Chap. 7.

32. Flobert, *Les Comores*, p. 97.

33. Jean Martin, "Une visite de la reine de Mohéli à Paris," *Bulletin de la société de l'Afrique Orientale* (POUNT) 8 (1967), pp. 29–40.

34. Said Bakari, *Swahili Chronicle of Ngazidja*, Lyndon Harries, ed., cyclostyled (Boston: Boston University, 1967). A new edition of this is forthcoming.

35. For events in Grande Comore see Dubins, "A Political History of the Comoro Islands," Chap. 8; Flobert, *Les Comores*; M. Fontoynant and E. Raomandahy, *La Grande Comore*, Mémoires de l'Académie Malgache, fascicule 22 (Tananarive, 1937); Faurec, *L'Archipel des sultans batailleurs*.

36. The text of this absurd concession is printed in Nicolas Du Plantier, *La Grande Comore* (Paris: Ministère des Colonies, 1904), pp. 44–45.

37. The best account of these events is given in Flobert, *Les Comores*, pp. 110–155. Also see Ali Saleh, "La France et la pacification de la Grande Comore," *Le Mois en Afrique* Nos. 196–197 (1982), pp. 113–131.

38. For Anjouan in the time of Sunley see Dubins, "A Political History of the Comoro Islands," Chap. 5; and R. Coupland, *The Exploitation of East Africa* (London: Faber and Faber, 1939).

39. Jean Martin, "Les Débuts du protectorat et la revolte servile de 1891 dans l'île d'Anjouan," *Revue française d'histoire d'outre-mer*, 1 trimestre (1973), pp. 45–85.

40. An account of Anjouan in 1901 was published by Jules Repiquet, *Le Sultanat d'Anjouan* (Paris, 1901); and a detailed account of the sultanate and its history is given by Völtzkow in *Die Comoren*, following his visit to the island in 1903.

41. The semi-servile condition of most of the population of Grande Comore and their obligation to work for the French is made a major attraction in Du Plantier's account of the island. See Du Plantier, *La Grande Comore*, pp. 30–31.

42. G. Lavau, "Les Comores," *La revue de Madagascar*, April (1934), p. 131.

43. Flobert, *Les Comores*, pp. 107, 150–153.

44. V. Thompson and R. Adloff, *The Malagasy Republic* (Stanford: Stanford University Press, 1965), pp. 49, 169, 271.

45. For the campaign in Madagascar see S. W. Roskill, *The War at Sea 1939–45*, 2 vols. (London: HMSO, 1956), vol. 2, pp. 185–192.

3

Comorian Politics

PARTI VERT AND PARTI BLANC

After World War II the French began to cultivate actively in their African colonies a class of *assimilés*—men on whom more and more local authority, and ultimately independence, could be devolved without the sacrifice of essential French strategic and economic interests. The Comoros, one of the least of the French territories, was to experience these changes along with the greatest. In 1946 the islands were declared to be a *territoire d'outre-mer* (*TOM*) and an elected conseil général, presided over by prince Said Hussein, a son of Said Ali, was established to advise the high commissioner. In 1947 the administration and finances of the Comoros were made separate from those of Madagascar, and in 1952 a separate customs regime was established. The French authorities in Madagascar retained overall authority until the final severance of all official ties in 1960, but to all intents and purposes the Comoros reverted to being a separate entity in 1946.

The real symbol of this new status was the right to send a deputy and a senator to the French National Assembly. The first deputy to be elected (by means of an electoral college) was Said Mohammed Cheik, who was to dominate Comorian politics until his death in 1970. Said Mohammed Cheik was typical of the men the French encouraged to come forward as heirs of direct colonial rule. He was descended on both sides from the ruling nobility of Grande Comore and was the first Comorian to qualify as a doctor. A political grouping, which became known as the parti vert—the Green party—developed around him. Like many other Comorian notables of his generation, Said Mohammed Cheik was a strong Gaullist, and one historian has even compared him, on his own minuscule political stage, with de Gaulle: "At this time people spoke of 'cheikism,' a phenomenon related to Gaullism through its character of being at the same time charismatic, authoritarian and popular."[1]

Said Mohammed Cheik used his lone voice in Paris with discretion and with some effect. He was able to draw the attention of French politicians to the neglected state of the islands. In 1949 came a measure of land reform, and in 1950, for the first time, France provided substantial aid after a cyclone devastated the archipelago. In 1948 the French agency for the distribution of aid (FIDES) initiated the first five-year plan, and a cautious and limited program of public works was begun.

In opposition to Said Mohammed Cheik, a rival grouping—called parti blanc, or the White party—formed around prince Said Ibrahim (another son of Said Ali—the last Sultan Thibé of Grande Comore—and brother of prince Said Hussein, who was the first president of the conseil général and one of the richest landowners in the south of Grande Comore). Throughout the 1950s Said Ibrahim unsuccessfully challenged Said Mohammed Cheik for the right to represent the islands in the French National Assembly, and antagonism between White and Green persisted until 1960, when the Comoros were permitted to send a second deputy and the two leaders agreed to share the honors. Since that time the rivalry between White and Green has tended to surface in Comorian politics whenever events split the united front that the ruling elite has tried to maintain in recent years.

What it was that divided White and Green is somewhat elusive. It has been suggested that the distinction was one of class: "the opposition of the commercial bourgeoisie—favoured by the administration—to the traditional aristocracy."[2] However, another political analyst described the partisans of the prince (White) as "in particular the large merchants" and those of the doctor (Green) as "essentially functionaries."[3] The distinction between White and Green did not derive in any clear-cut manner from island or clan rivalries. Both leaders had their power bases on Grande Comore, and each counted members of the same families among his followers. Nor did ideology appear to count at this stage, for both were equally pro-French, and the near unanimity in the voting on the referendum in 1958 shows that there was no division of opinion on policy.

The reality is that during the 1940s and 1950s political parties comprised the personal followings of individual leaders. As Said Mohammed Cheik was in a position to dispense a certain amount of patronage, it is not surprising that his following included the petty fonctionnaires of the colonial regime. Nor is it surprising that prince Said Ibrahim attracted those among the leading families who felt themselves out of power. Once changes in the constitution opened an official role for the prince as well as the doctor, the antagonism of White and Green subsided, and common electoral fronts were adopted. "This reconciliation of Whites and Greens sounded the knell of struggles which had been due only to personality problems."[4] When political factionalism surfaced again in 1968, it was no longer just personalities that divided Comorians but a variety of increasingly urgent political decisions.

THE ROAD TO SELF-GOVERNMENT

In 1956 the French socialist government of Guy Mollet passed the *loi cadre* that established the constitutional framework by which the French African territories would evolve constitutionally as separate entities and not as parts of a larger federal structure. The *loi cadre* established universal suffrage in the Comoros and made provision for the election of a territorial assembly with powers to vote on the budget. The conseil général became a conseil du gouvernement presided over by a French administrateur supérieur. Each island became an administrative circumscription with its own assembly but was administered by a prefect. The conseil du gouvernement received some executive powers, but this was to prove a mere hors d'oeuvre before the constitutional feast that was to follow. The Fourth Republic was tottering to its fall, and with the accession of de Gaulle to power in 1958 the colonies were given the opportunity to vote on their future constitutional relationship with France.[5]

Said Mohammed Cheik believed, with some justification, that the Comoros would be defenseless if they were cut off from France and would not have the economic resources or the necessary skills to survive as an independent state. He publicly opposed the objective of independence for the Comoros and urged the electorate to vote for the status of *territoire d'outre-mer* instead. Such status would allow the archipelago to achieve responsible government under the protection of France and with full French cooperation.

The referendum was held in September 1958 and proved an overwhelming triumph for the political skills of Said Mohammed Cheik: 92.7 percent of the electorate voted, and of that 97.3 percent voted for the status of *TOM*. In December the territorial assembly confirmed this verdict by voting twenty-five to four to accept *TOM* status—the four votes in opposition cast by the deputies from Mayotte. Majorities of this kind were to be common in future Comorian elections, and it must be assumed that considerable administrative attention was devoted to achieving such a favorable result. Nevertheless, there is no reason to assume at this stage that, Mayotte apart, the majority of Comorians did not trust the policy recommended to them by Said Mohammed Cheik.[6]

The task now was to negotiate full responsible government. This took patience and skill, for de Gaulle was having to reassess the direction of his whole African policy and accept a scaling-down of his ambitions for a French African community. With Madagascar pressing for full independence and achieving it in 1960, France's position in the Indian Ocean seemed at risk, and it was reluctant to make concessions to the Comorians that would significantly lessen French control. Nevertheless, after being three times modified in negotiation, a new constitution was granted in 1961. The new structure of power allowed for a French high commissioner, who would handle all external relations, defense, and the affairs of the franc zone; an elected chambre des députés and a conseil du gouvernement; and a president elected by the deputies to preside over the conseil. In practice the constitutional relationship between the islands and France remained obscure, and nominal responsible government did not amount to very much in the face of the overwhelming dependence on France that remained.

There was only one serious candidate for the prestigious new post of president, and Said Mohammed Cheik was duly chosen to become the first elected head of state of the Comoros. Ever since the path toward responsible government had been mapped out in 1956, the rival parties of Green and White had tended to bury their differences, a process made easier when Said Ibrahim was elected as the islands' second deputy to the French assembly. France must have felt it had successfully installed a Francophile, assimilé government that would help to safeguard its interests in the western Indian Ocean. Real power still lay with the high commissioner, and the coming together of the two factions among the notables promised to stifle political debate and demands for more radical change. For the French the stability of the regime was proved in 1965 when the Comorians were called upon to vote in the French presidential elections. The traditional Gaullism of the Comorian leaders secured 99.4 percent of the poll for the general, with a mere 0.58 percent voting for his socialist rival, François Mitterrand. In the Comorian elections of 1967 Green and White came together to fight on a common coalition ticket.[7]

Across the Mozambique Channel, however, radical change was taking place. Tanganyika became independent and adopted development policies based on concepts of African socialism. In Zanzibar, the country closest to the Comoros in social and economic structure, a bloody revolution overthrew the dominant Arab ruling class in 1964. In the same year Mozambican nationalists began an armed insurrection against the Portuguese, and the United Nations and the Organization of African Unity became major platforms for the discussion of colonial issues. The emotions of independence politics did not pass the Comoros by but rather distracted the attention of politicians, tempting them to ignore for too long, and with ultimately disastrous results, the political developments in Mayotte.

MAYOTTE SEPARATISM

Mayotte had been directly administered by France since the 1840s, some sixty years before French rule was established elsewhere in the archipelago. In the twentieth century the French administration had maintained the capital of the islands on the tiny, waterless rock of Dzaoudzi, which had originally been chosen because its guns could dominate the lagoon. The inappropriateness of having a capital on Dzaoudzi must be emphasized. The rocky island is circular and less

than half a mile wide. In 1960 it contained a barracks for the Foreign
Legion, a church, a military hospital, and a hotel. In addition, there
were three or four French houses, a small school, an Indian store, and
one range of administrative buildings. These structures all dated from
the nineteenth century and by the middle of the twentieth century were
in a state of picturesque decay. Overshadowed by coconut palms and
with the great naval guns rusting on their mountings, the whole island
had become a symbol of a forgotten, decaying colonialism. Nineteenth-
century plans to move the capital to the mainland at Mamoutzou had
come to nothing, but Dzaoudzi had been connected by a causeway with
nearby Pamanzi Island, and it was there that an airstrip was built and
some French creoles put up houses. Even after the passing of the *loi
cadre*, the French administration continued to reside at Dzaoudzi, and
the conseil du gouvernement met there.

Although the French invested little in the islands before the 1960s,
there is no doubt that Mayotte benefited most from what official
expenditure did take place; French officers and *fonctionnaires* came and
went, and the units of the Legion spent some of their pay. Moreover,
there were always some French who settled near the capital, married
local women, and helped to swell the tiny, but vocal, creole class. In
1958, however, the new government of the islands decided to move the
administrative capital. A site at Patsy on Anjouan was proposed, but
in the end the decision fell on Moroni. The territorial assembly already
met there, and the town had the advantage of being the political power
base of Said Mohammed Cheik. In the end it was his influence that
led to the transfer of the capital from waterless Dzaoudzi to the equally
waterless old Arab town of Moroni.

The actual change took place in 1962 after the grant of responsible
government. However, by this time a strong Mayotte separatist movement
had already begun.[8] In November 1958 a Congrès des Notables de
Mayotte was summoned by Georges Nahouda to protest against the
movement of the capital and also to press for full departmental status
for the Comoros—in other words, for full integration into France. It
included the four deputies from Mayotte who had already voted against
acceptance of *TOM* status.

The organization of the Mouvement Mahorais (MM), the political
party that has continued to dominate Mayotte politics, only took place
after the transfer of the capital. It was started in 1966 by Zeina M'Dere,
a Comorian woman from Madagascar, who obtained impressive backing
from the women in the neighborhood of Dzaoudzi who were particularly
affected economically by the departure of so many of the French. At
first the male Mayotte deputies took a back seat in the Mouvement,
and it was the women who organized popular demonstrations. By the
mid-1960s, however, the Mouvement was increasingly becoming the
political tool of the creole Henry family. There was considerable personal
hostility between Marcel Henry and Said Mohammed Cheik. In 1966

Said Mohammed tried to visit Mayotte, but a large demonstration was organized against him, and stones were thrown. Said Mohammed then decided to punish Mayotte, starving it of government funds, withdrawing the only doctor from the islands, and refusing to provide a ferry to link the smaller islands with the Mayotte mainland.[9]

This attitude allowed Henry to consolidate his power on the island, and in the elections of 1967 he obtained 95 percent of the vote for his list. The fact that the Henry family was creole was significant. The Mayotte creoles were very few in number, probably fewer than one hundred,[10] and they were a declining class. Many had had to abandon their old estates for lack of labor and capital. They were just the group to produce dissident, radical politicians. They found allies among the Malagasy-speaking islanders (a minority in the archipelago as a whole but strong on Mayotte) and were assisted by the absence of powerful male Muslim leadership. They were able to play on the resentment engendered by the removal of the capital and on the fears of many Mahorais that they would be dominated by Grande Comore, a fear that was focused immediately on the immigrants from Grande Comore who were settling on Mayotte. Henry made great play with the idea that the Mahorais were ethnically and culturally different from other Comorians—being Catholic, French-speaking, and of Malagasy origin, characteristics that were in fact, only possessed by a very small number of the Mahorais. He also developed the original demand for departmental status for the Comoros as a whole into a demand for separate departmental status for Mayotte itself.

If Henry's emotional hostility to Moroni assured him of popular support, his exaggerated pro-French stance proved to be very shrewd politically. In 1966, when the Mahorais rioted against the visit of the president, the French high commissioner refused to take action against crowds who were chanting *"vive la France"*; and the waving of the tricolor and the fancy expressions of loyalty to France have greatly helped the Mouvement Mahorais to get a hearing in Paris. The Mouvement certainly received general encouragement from French politicians of the right and implicit recognition even from the government, which in the new constitutional settlement of 1967 spoke of the need to "define the individuality and the personality of the different circumscriptions."[11] At the same time the Mouvement stimulated anti-French sentiment elsewhere in the archipelago and in particular anti-French suspicions among the ruling notables of Grande Comore and Anjouan. Anti-French sentiment was, however, being fed into the Comorian political bloodstream from other sources as well.

MOLINACO

If provincial, tribal, and communal separatism comprise one face of modern African politics, radical movements of the left comprise another. In 1963 the Mouvement pour la Libération Nationale des Comores (MOLINACO) was founded among Comorian exiles and residents in Dar es Salaam.[12] The movement was nurtured on the radicalism of Tanzania and Zanzibar and was given the use of a broadcasting station to spread its propaganda. From the outset it demanded the withdrawal of the French and instant independence—a message simple and clear enough to win approval in the Africa of the 1960s. As a result, MOLINACO, headed at the time by Abdou Bakara Boina, was recognized by the Organization of African Unity, which provided it with funds.

MOLINACO did not live up to the expectations of its sponsors. It failed to build a base within the islands, most of its attempts to do so being deliberately headed off by the French and their conservative allies among the islands' rulers. As a result, MOLINACO suffered the fate of many exile movements: It was branded as an "African" party, and the frustrations of always having to speak from exile led to splits in the party and a decline in its influence. It was not until 1972, for example, that the United Nations was persuaded to refer the future of the islands to the colonization committee, having previously accepted the French case that the islands had been granted self-determination in 1958.[13] In September of the same year MOLINACO set up a front organization, Parti pour l'Evolution des Comores (PEC), in Moroni to fight local elections. By that time MOLINACO had been upstaged by the traditional, conservative parties, which were also campaigning for independence, and PEC meekly agreed to enter into a coalition with the Whites and the Greens. It is not surprising that young radicals who had looked to MOLINACO in the early 1960s had already begun to show signs of placing their hopes elsewhere.

THE ROAD TO INDEPENDENCE

The constitutional arrangements of 1961 had proved satisfactory to France but not so satisfactory to the local politicians. Responsible government had turned out to be little more than a form of words, and the high commissioner, in fact, controlled the islands much as his predecessor, the administrateur supérieur, had done. As France made up the considerable budget deficits, provided investment funds, and controlled external relations and the defense forces, its word was, in practice, law. Although the ruling notables had been strongly Gaullist and pro-French, they had not been unaffected by the independence fever in Africa and increasingly leveled criticism at the economic backwardness of the islands. The moderate Said Ibrahim, for example, complained to Le Monde that although the Comoros made up half the population of all the French TOMs, they received only about 10 percent of the aid that France directed toward the TOMs.[14]

Fears that MOLINACO might gain influence in Comorian politics and resentment at the strident claims of the Mouvement Mahorais, which succeeded, after 1967, in making Mayotte virtually a "no-go" area for Moroni politicians, led Said Mohammed Cheik to press Paris for further concessions. In particular, he wanted a clearer definition of the respective powers of his government and the French high commissioner, a definition that would limit French interference in purely internal matters. Less French interference would help convince Comorian opinion of the reality of responsible government, but more importantly, it would give the president a freer hand in dealing with Mayotte. With the sweeping victory of the White and Green coalition in the 1967 elections the time seemed ripe for realizing some of the goodwill that Comorian support for General de Gaulle had banked in Paris.

Constitutional amendments eventually were passed by the French assembly in December 1967, but they did little more than update the arrangements of 1961.[15] The Comorian president was now made fully responsible for internal security, and greater independence in judicial matters was granted. However, these changes were scarcely adequate to satisfy the ideologies and aspirations of contemporary Africa. The fundamental relationships did not change. The Comoros remained wholly dependent, since France provided the funds to finance the budget, all investment capital, and the largest market for Comorian produce. Moreover, if the Comorian president had scarcely increased his power vis-à-vis France, he also had to contend with a formidable degree of decentralization in the local government of the archipelago itself. The French had insisted that each island form an administrative circumscription under a prefect nominated by the conseil du gouvernement. On Anjouan and Grande Comore there were also three subprefects. Each island had an elected assembly and a conseil du préfecture, while the larger towns were endowed with elected municipal councils. Such a structure of local government gave every opportunity for the Mayotte separatists to enjoy virtual autonomy, and these provisions were seen as a gesture of support for their aspirations.

The passage of the constitutional amendments had scarcely taken place when Moroni experienced a major internal crisis. A crash at the city's airport had led to confusion among the would-be rescuers and to allegations of pillage. The students of the *lycée*, which was situated near the airport, staged a strike and demonstrations, which were violently repressed by the police in March 1968. The disorders broke the confidence of the ruling coalition, and in April Said Mohammed Cheik resigned. Said Ibrahim was willing to see deeper causes in the unrest when he told *Le Monde* that *"la crise politique est due pour une bonne part aux difficultés économiques."*[16]

Said Mohammed Cheik formed another government but the old coalition between Whites and Greens was not reconstituted. In September 1968 Said Mohammed Djaffa, a French senator and nephew and son-in-law of Said Ibrahim, created the Rassemblement Démocratique des Peuples Comoriens (RDPC). The RDPC was based on Grande Comore,

Mitsamiouli: Political comment on the walls of a closed hospital

and an allied party, the Parti Social Démocratique des Comores (PSDC), appeared on Anjouan under the leadership of Ali Mirghane. It soon became apparent that the RDPC and its allies were the old White party under a new name. The old Green alliance also reappeared in the form of a party called UDC (Union Démocratique des Comores), which enjoyed the fruits of Said Mohammed Cheik's last years in office.

The founding of these two parties in 1968 was not just a revival of past factionalism but reflected a sharpening political conflict. The RDPC, although still recognizing the conservative Said Ibrahim as leader, began to advocate increasingly the need for economic and social reform, questioning the role of the French plantation companies and the existing land regime. The UDC, on the other hand, received a lot of political support on Anjouan, and after the death of Said Mohammed Cheik it came to be dominated by the Anjouan notables. The rivalry of RDPC (White) and UDC (Green) then became more explicitly a rivalry between Grande Comore and Anjouan. However, it is important not to make too much of these ideological and island rivalries. Both parties were split internally on the vital political issue of independence, and the RDPC was able to find support on Anjouan behind the façade of the locally based PSDC.

On March 16, 1970, Said Mohammed Cheik, the respected father of Comorian politics, died. He had sought to maintain a broad coalition among the Comorian ruling notables based on close ties with France and cautious steps toward greater internal political autonomy. The economic backwardness of the archipelago was recognized, but the interests of the wealthy supporters of the regime dictated that the only practical solution to that backwardness should be economic aid from France and investment by French capital. The president had maintained his position throughout the 1960s, when Africa was going through the revolutionary changes of independence, but by 1968 his act was visibly wearing thin. His relations with Mayotte had proved a major failure, and it was clear that some of the White and Green notables were finding the prospect of independence attractive as a means of upstaging more radical political voices and so retaining their own power. At his death the president's own UDC party was deeply divided on the independence issue. Finally, Said Mohammed Cheik had failed to attract the allegiance of the younger generation.

PASOCO AND THE EMERGENCE OF RADICAL POLITICS

One of the by-products of the disorders of 1968 had been the founding of the Parti Socialiste des Comores (PASOCO).[17] PASOCO had its origins in an association called ASEC (Association des Stagiaires et Etudiants Comoriens) founded among Comorian students in France in 1966. Many of these students were from wealthy Comorian families, and at first it seemed as if this group would be as remote from the ordinary Comorian peasant as was MOLINACO. The events of 1968, however, gave the socialist leaders of PASOCO an opportunity to establish a base inside the country, and PASOCO soon became a party of the younger generation. In particular, PASOCO found support on Grande Comore, where the *lycée* was situated, and on Mohéli, which had become increasingly isolated in Comorian politics and was beginning to show the first signs of political awareness.

PASOCO was closely watched by the authorities, but although it suffered a certain amount of harassment, it was tolerated and was even allowed to advertise its presence in a modest way. This tolerance may at first appear surprising, but perhaps the explanation lies in the fact that PASOCO was not the chosen instrument of the Organization of African Unity and was in fact challenging MOLINACO for radical support. While PASOCO might have the effect of weakening its rival, it did not seem to pose any electoral threat to the established parties—a supposition that was borne out when PASOCO put up a list of candidates in the 1972 elections. On that occasion it polled only 3.5 percent of the vote on Grande Comore but a significant 23 percent on Mohéli. In 1971 PASOCO was seriously weakened by the desertion of its treasurer, Ali Himidi, to the UDC.[18]

In spite of these setbacks PASOCO was able to build up its organization in the years preceding the 1975 declaration of independence. It was able to stage demonstrations, and when Bernard Stasi, the French minister for *DOM/TOM* (Départments d'Outre Mer and Territoires d'Outre Mer), visited Moroni in September 1973 he was met at the airport with a vigorous demonstration demanding independence. In the meantime PASOCO had established branches in the main towns and built up support by holding social events with music and refreshments for young people in different parts of the islands. Most significantly it began to produce a paper, which was called *Uhuru*. This sole representative of the free press in the Comoros was cyclostyled, as was the official government information bulletin *Info'Comore*, for there was at that time no printing press of any description in the islands. *Uhuru* appeared weekly in an edition of 500, and its well-thumbed copies circulated clandestinely. As suited a revolutionary journal, *Uhuru* was more distinguished for its political zeal than for the artistry of its layout. It contained articles on current affairs, seriously researched pieces on the society and economy of the islands, and a gossip column aimed at exposing the corruption and hypocrisy of Comorian public life. In many of the editions the jargon lay as thickly on the pages as it no doubt did in the notebooks of the economics students who wrote it, but for the most part the authors were well informed about the social and economic problems of their society, and their criticisms were often both trenchant and relevant.

Much of *Uhuru's* stock-in-trade consisted of slogans that could mean anything to the reader, such as "the future of the Comoros is linked to the capacity of the people to become masters of their own destiny" and "all true patriots should unite their efforts to defeat the designs of French colonialism and local reaction." However, the journal had much more punch when it talked about economics: for example, "After 130 years of French colonialism the Comoros do not possess an economy even on the way to development."[19] And *Uhuru* went on to criticize current aid programs for merely swelling the bureaucracy. When PASOCO got down to being practical, Tanzanian self-help was clearly the model that it adopted, as exemplified by the following statements: "Our point of departure will be the experiments of the *Ujamaa* villages" and "one can plan or attempt to plan an autocentric development policy financed by national means. One cannot plan a development which depends entirely on foreign capital and external demands."[20]

The advocacy of self-help naturally led the journal to attack aspects of Comorian society that appeared to stand in the way of the reorganization of society. In particular the *grand mariage*, with its conspicuous consumption and assertion of social hierarchy, came in for criticism. Similarly the traditional social and class divisions that dominated island politics were treated to orthodox Marxist analysis, and *Uhuru* pressed for immediate independence from France because, among other things, that would expose the class conflict in the islands without the complication of colonial overrule.

SAID IBRAHIM IN POWER

With the departure of Said Mohammed Cheik there was only one man with the political stature and experience—not to speak of the requisite French goodwill—to take over the government. In September 1970 Prince Said Ibrahim, the White leader, became president,[21] a position he was to occupy in a well-meaning but indecisive manner for the next two years.

It is clear that in pressing its demands for independence PASOCO had been speaking for more and more Comorians. The traditional parties found they had to take a stance on this issue, which they found deeply divisive. The Whites were the immediate beneficiaries of this situation. With their rivals split on the independence issue, they were able to carry twenty-one of the seats in the assembly (now raised to a total of thirty-nine) when elections were held in June 1971. In spite of this success Said Ibrahim was increasingly trying to rule above party. He appointed men of all factions, and in his effort to create a political consensus he made a serious attempt to solve the Mayotte problem. He entered into a political alliance with the Mouvement Mahorais and appointed Marcel Henry's brother, Martial Henry, to his cabinet, in this way trying to bring Mayotte back into the mainstream of Comorian political life.[22]

Said Ibrahim and the Henry family shared one political objective— they were anxious to head off independence from France. The president himself firmly opposed independence, partly out of long-standing pro-French sentiment but also because, as he realistically said, *"il n'y a pas d'indépendance politique sans indépendance économique."*[23] The Comoros, he believed, would remain wholly dependent on French aid whether formal independence was granted or not. Said Ibrahim did not, however, follow Henry's desire for integration as a French department, and he began to speak the language of gradualism, relegating independence to an undefined and misty future. In this he was more and more at odds with the other White leaders.

Although he had won an election as recently as June 1971, Said Ibrahim was forced to resign in October 1972 by a new grouping of politicians, drawn from both RDPC (Whites) and UDC (Greens), who installed Said Mohammed Djaffa as president pending new elections. The independence issue had led to Said Ibrahim's fall. The Comorian notables were alarmed at what appeared to be France's new attitude toward the future of the islands. Since 1912 there had never been any question about the political unity of the four islands, but in the constitutional reforms of 1967 France had insisted on strengthening the individual island governments at the expense of the Moroni administration. Then, in 1972, Pierre Mesmer, then minister for *DOM/TOM*, had visited the archipelago and had assured Mayotte politicians that "nothing would be done without a referendum in which each island would be called upon to decide its own future." He also said that the results of the referendum would be announced island by island, and "each island that voted against independence would continue to form part of the French *ensemble*."[24] This statement seemed to be a perfectly clear signal to Mayotte politicians to persist in their opposition to Moroni, and the fragmentation of the archipelago was clearly envisaged.

The new White and Green coalition, formed to fight on a platform of independence, significantly adopted the name *Unité*, encapsulating their opposition to the threatened breakup of the archipelago. In the elections held in December 1972 the coalition was joined by MOLINACO and won every seat in the assembly except those allotted to Mayotte. Said Ibrahim had formed his own party, Umma, to fight the election and to oppose independence, but its only support came from Grande Comore, where it polled 23 percent of the vote. The new government was headed by Ahmed Abdullah, who took office with a clear mandate to seek independence for a united Comoro state.[25]

AHMED ABDULLAH AND
THE DECLARATION OF INDEPENDENCE

Ahmed Abdullah was a politician of a different stamp from his aristocratic predecessors. He had made a fortune in vanilla exporting and rice importing, and he had wide connections in the business world. Also unlike his predecessors, his political power base was on Anjouan, where numerous houses belonging to his wives and members of his family testified to his wealth and influence and where he had the unique ability to attract votes from both town and country. Ahmed Abdullah, having sat in the French senate since 1962, had considerable political experience, but his political style was very much his own. *Uhuru* was at its best lampooning the new president as a "hand-shaking" politician at pains to cultivate followers by paying them personal attentions. A phrase current in Mayotte at that time referred to a government supporter as a *serrer-la-main*, a hand-shaker. Abdullah's style was in other ways more brash and bourgeois than Said Mohammed Cheik's had been. He was probably the only head of state in the world who, instead of supplying a dignified portrait photograph to adorn government offices, printed a calendar advertising "Ahmed Abdullah, import and export agent."[26]

Abdullah realized that unless the ruling notables of the islands adopted a more aggressive attitude toward the French and their colonial system, they would lose the support of public opinion to the nationalists of MOLINACO or to the socialists of PASOCO; the fate of the Arab ruling class of Zanzibar was only too clearly in his mind. He was also politician enough to see the political advantages of independence in terms of approval from fellow African heads of state and of the pickings to be obtained from participation in international commissions, conferences, etc. He may also have believed that France would have to bid higher for the support of an independent Comoros and that French aid would increase rather than diminish as a result. However, what probably pushed him rapidly into action was the Mayotte problem and the fear that France was trying to detach the island from the Comoros as a whole.

Independence, it was believed, would check France's ambitions with regard to Mayotte, for independence in Africa had always been based on the principle of the integrity of colonial frontiers. However, Mahorais separatism also had to be tackled at the grass roots. Abdullah attacked the Mayotte question with subtlety and some success. In 1972 a rival to the Mouvement Mahorais called L'Union des Jeunes pour le Progrès de Mayotte was founded. It was able to tap a fount of opposition to Henry and his clan, and in the December 1972 elections Henry, who had managed 99 percent of the vote in 1971, saw his percentage reduced to 80 percent.[27] Then, Ahmed Abdullah encouraged the preaching of a conservative sheikh, Said Ali Vita, who played on Islamic resentment at the dominance of Christian creoles and on the traditional male opposition to the role being played in Mayotte politics by women. At the same time the migration of peasants from Anjouan and Grande Comore, which had begun as a movement of seasonal workers, was officially encouraged. So successful were these policies that when the next test of the ballot box occurred in the 1974 French presidential elections, only 60 percent of the electorate followed Henry's advice to vote for Giscard.[28]

Abdullah began to negotiate independence from France at once. In June 1973 he returned from Paris with further constitutional concessions and with the promise of a referendum on independence in the next five years. In November he received clear evidence of the head of steam building up behind the independence issue when a pro-independence riot in Moroni led to the burning of the buildings of the chambre des députés and the necessity of declaring martial law.[29] At the same time a new opposition party was formed around Said Ibrahim's Umma, which called itself the Front National Uni (FNU) and which, rather incongruously, included PASOCO. The leaders of the new party were Said Ibrahim and his protégé, agronomist Ali Soilih, a rising political star. The party itself presented the extraordinary sight of a coalition of moderate traditionalists and left-wing radicals and is yet one more indication of the small extent to which ideology appeared to matter in Comorian politics in comparison with personality.

The holding of the referendum assured that for the first time Comorian affairs would attract more than a passing interest from the metropolitan politicians. The French government was probably prepared to consult the Comorian people as a whole and was strongly supported in this by the Communists. However, many of the opposition groups rallied behind the idea of a consultation on an island-by-island basis that would have the effect of fully exposing the pro-French sentiments of Mayotte. In the end, defeated on this issue in the Senate, the president announced a *"consultation des populations"* instead of a *"consultation de la population."* The referendum on independence was held on December 22, 1974 after Giscard had been understood to commit France to abide by the result. The outcome was 95 percent support for independence, the only opposition coming from Mayotte, where Henry managed to get a much-curtailed majority against independence—the voting on Mayotte being 5,110 for and 8,783 against. The decisive nature of Abdullah's "yes" vote was very much in line with other electoral victories in modern Comorian history, and its achievement required a great deal of administrative resourcefulness, or so the Mouvement Mahorais alleged.[30]

The aftermath of the referendum left France undecided about policy. Eventually a parliamentary delegation went to the Comoros, and its report led to the suggestion that a constitutional conference should be held and that independence should be postponed until a new constitution could be accepted by each island in yet another referendum. With these blatant delaying tactics the French succeeded in driving Ahmed Abdullah into a corner. Suspicions were voiced about his real commitment to independence, and his whole political credibility seemed to be at stake.

It was hardly a well-thought-out move by France. Ahmed Abdullah was just the sort of politician the French should have been happy to see in charge of a newly independent Comoros. With his extensive business interests he was the ideal leader to keep the islands safe for French economic and strategic interests. The Mouvement Mahorais, on the other hand, offered little political advantage for France. Its hold on Mayotte was weakening, and it had no standing at all outside the island. Yet, there was a feeling of unease in France at the idea of abandoning altogether a military presence in the Mozambique Channel. This uneasiness was played upon by the traditional Gaullists led by the deputy for Réunion, Michel Debré, who was in a good position to claim to speak for the "Gaullist" Mahorais as well. Although the French president had appeared to commit himself to a united Comoros in the autumn of 1974, the right was able to achieve a majority in favor of postponement when the matter was eventually debated in June 1975. This last-minute attempt to evade the granting of independence is the sort of action taken by politicians who are not well enough informed about an issue to make sound decisions.[31]

Urged on by strong popular sentiment and by politicians of all parties, Abdullah declared the islands independent of France on July 6, 1975. The Mayotte deputies were absent, and the Mouvement Mahorais promptly stated that the island of Mayotte would remain French. Independence, which had been promoted out of fear for the unity of the archipelago, precipitated, as its first result, the very breakup it had been designed to prevent.

ALI SOILIH'S REVOLUTIONARY STATE

On August 3, 1975, less than a month after his declaration of independence, a coup toppled Ahmed Abdullah from power. The leaders of the coup were soon seen to be familiar figures—the leaders of the old White party—and the coup itself appeared to be just another swing of the political pendulum of Comorian factionalism. For the second time, Said Mohammed Djaffa, the man who had held power briefly in 1972 before the election of Ahmed Abdullah, was chosen as interim president. Behind him, however, there were other men, notably Ali Soilih. The old White leader, Said Ibrahim, did not take office himself but remained in the background as a revered figurehead.

At first it was widely assumed that France had engineered the coup, for the new leaders were well-known moderates who had belonged to the faction that had opposed independence.[32] Said Mohammed Djaffa himself probably believed that France would react favorably to the new regime and that the problem of Mayotte would be quickly settled, with France happy to see it rejoin an independent but francophile Comoro Republic. In the meantime, however, Ahmed Abdullah's power base on Anjouan had to be brought to heel, and this was achieved by sending to the island a small armed force led by a group of French mercenaries. When discussions with France over the constitutional positon of the islands were held in October, however, French policy took a hard line over Mayotte. France recognized the independence of three of the islands and declared a consultative referendum for Mayotte. Ali Soilih went to Mayotte to try to assert Moroni's authority on the island, but the French allowed a mob, raised by the Mouvement Mahorais, to oppose him at the airport, and he returned humiliated. At the end of the year the situation was exacerbated when the Mahorais leaders proceeded to expel "foreign" elements from Mayotte—in practice, to purge the island of their opponents. In February 1976 the French duly conducted a referendum in Mayotte, the result being a 99.4 percent vote in favor of remaining French. When a similar vote had been taken in December 1974, only 64 percent had voted against independence and to remain French. The near unanimity achieved in 1976 was a measure of the

extent to which the Mouvement Mahorais had regained control of the
islands' politics and, one must assume, of the machinery for organizing
elections. In April a further vote was taken to decide on the exact status
of the island, and an overwhelming 97.46 percent of the votes cast
demanded acceptance as a full department. This result, however, was
marred, as far as the Mouvement Mahorais was concerned, by the fact
that only just over 20 percent of the electorate voted.[33]

France's snubbing of the moderate leaders of the coup against
Abdullah and allowing the Mouvement Mahorais a free hand in developing the island's separatism are difficult to reconcile with any rational
assessment of France's long-term interests. One view is that France was
anxious not to lose the option of developing a military base on Mayotte
after ending the French military presence in Madagascar in 1972, but
Mayotte was not turned into a base. A more plausible explanation
attributes the French activity to the political influence wielded by
politicians from Réunion.[34] Certainly, after the separation of Mayotte
from the Comoros there was a great growth of Réunion business activity
on the island. However, if French behavior throughout this crisis is not
easily explained, the effects that flowed from it are clear enough. The
resentment and disillusionment of the regime on Moroni was profound.
In November 1975 it began to pursue a strongly anti-French policy that
eventually led it to try to sever all ties with and dependence on France.
This entailed nothing less than a total revolution.

On January 2, 1976, the Comorian chamber of deputies voted Said
Mohammed Djaffa out of office and replaced him with Ali Soilih. Soilih
was thirty-nine at the time of the coup and was a politician of a new
stamp.[35] He did not come from a noble family and had been brought
up in a rural area of Grande Comore. He won his way to an education
in France, where he trained as an agronomist, and served as a minister
with Said Ibrahim between 1970 and 1972, joining his mentor to form
the Umma party in autumn of that year. He had already defied the
conservative mores of the country in a significant way by refusing to
contract a *grand mariage,* and he approached the islands' problems with
the outlook of an economist and an intellectual, not a member of the
traditional elite. He had frequently gone on record as saying that there
would have to be a radical restructuring of social and economic institutions
and that as long as the present hierarchy and scale of values existed
in the country there could not be any progress. It is wrong, however,
to see him as a revolutionary burning with hatred for the established
order. It is generally accepted that he remained close to Said Ibrahim
and that the latter's death on a pilgrimage in December 1975 removed
a significant moderating influence in his life. *"Cette disparition prive Ali
Soilih d'une caution morale irremplaçable dans un système politique encore
féodale,"* as the most recent historian of the Comoros has written.[36]

Soilih, however, did not immediately initiate the class revolution
that the previous example of Zanzibar suggested might occur. He began

by welcoming into his government men from many different political backgrounds: former Green politicians, MOLINACO supporters, and men with Umma and White pedigrees. Ahmed Abdullah was allowed to leave the islands with a diplomatic passport, and Soilih even enlisted the support of M. Lègres, the leading French businessman in Grande Comore. However, this "united front" began to crumble in April 1976 with the discovery of an alleged plot against Soilih involving some of his closest colleagues. Even then the development of the revolutionary regime was gradual, very patchy in its effects, and extremely moderate by the standards of other self-professed revolutions.

Whatever intellectuals like to imagine, "revolutionary" regimes are seldom made according to blueprints, Marxist or otherwise. Like the programs of all political regimes they take form as a result of the interaction of immediate problems and events on minds already conditioned by ideology and accustomed to thinking in a certain way. Soilih's revolution was no exception, being impelled on its way by a series of pressing day-to-day problems. The failure of negotiations with France in October 1975 and the abortive attempt to regain Mayotte had led France to adopt toward the errant little republic the same attitude adopted by de Gaulle toward Guinée in 1958. France suspended all aid and withdrew almost all its technical personnel. Suddenly, the Comorian state was without any senior civil servants, without an army, without technicians, without teachers for the *lycée* or *collèges*, without doctors, and above all, without the finances that made up three-quarters of the budget and paid for all the development programs.[37]

An urgent task, therefore, was to build a system of international alliances that would replace the technical and financial aid no longer supplied by France. Soilih approached the Organization of African Unity, the Arab League, the Soviet Union, China, and then various francophone countries such as Canada, Switzerland, Belgium, and even Haiti. At first the new regime found friends everywhere. China opened a diplomatic mission, Senegal agreed to act as mediator with France, and technical personnel were sent by a number of countries. However, this promising international initiative faltered by the end of 1976 as the internal chaos in the islands grew and the inability of the regime to cope with even the most basic administrative matters became clear.

Meanwhile, young Comorians, who clearly formed the basis of Soilih's support, were taking over the ministries and agencies vacated by the French; a new defense force was being organized by officers seconded from Tanzania; and a state company was set up to handle vital imports and exports. To build solid support for his regime, Ali Soilih encouraged youth groups to take political and administrative initiatives, and in August 1976 he summoned an assembly in Moroni to propose a program of vital economic reforms. By the end of the year all practical restraint on Soilih's young revolutionaries seemed to have been removed, and with little or no central control or direction, they were taking over power at the local level from the village headmen and urban notables. Armed bands, known as *commandos Moissi*, were formed to enforce adherence to the ideals of the new regime.[38] These ideals were clearly based on the ideas that had been voiced by PASOCO, but they were expressed largely through symbols: the wearing of the veil by women was prohibited, quite as much because it was a symbol of class superiority as because it represented Islamic subjection of women; the *grand mariage* was outlawed, as were Islamic funerals; the activities of the *imams* and *mwalimus* were curtailed; and local notables were pressed into gangs working on public works. Some people no doubt "disappeared," but in general the terror of the *Moissi* gangs bore little resemblance to the revolutionary terrors of Zanzibar or of other revolutionary regimes.

Events pushed Soilih and his followers into more extreme and more radical postures. At the end of December 1976 there was a massacre of Comorians in Majunga, Madagascar, in which at least 1,400 lost their lives. When the violence died down, the decision was taken to evacuate as much of the long-settled Comorian population on Madagascar as possible. During 1977 possibly as many as 17,000 people sought repatriation. A further unforeseen event was the violent eruption of the Karthala Volcano during April 1977, which left up to 2,000 people homeless on Grande Comore and resulted in massive destruction of plantations and agriculture. Crisis only intensified Soilih's desire to rush through change.[39]

In April 1977 events were staged that will always give the Comorian revolution a niche in historical memory. On April 12, the central government machinery was disbanded and eleven ministries were closed. Up to 3,500 civil servants were told to return to their homes, Ali Soilih himself symbolically returning to the village of his birth. The archives of the government were then burnt. Ten days later, on April 23, the *loi fondamentale* was published, implementing a new administrative order that was to be totally decentralized. Thirty-four moudiryias were to be created, each with a population of about 9,000. The moudiryias were to be headed by a judge and were to be the basic unit for the organization of education, food supplies, and security. Priority was to be given to the construction of primary schools and public administrative buildings within the moudiryia. The moudiryias themselves were grouped in seven prefectures.[40]

At the center of affairs was to be an eleven-man conseil d'état and a national assembly. Gradually, however, a new central administration had to be created, and by the end of 1977 four rudimentary ministries had appeared to handle foreign affairs, finance, development, and security. The new constitution, which defined the state as a *république démocratique, laïque, et sociale*, was put to the people in a referendum in October 1977 and approved by a precarious 55 percent. This majority, so uncharacteristically low for a Comorian election, can be seen as a measure of the relative honesty of the regime or, more cynically, as evidence of its lack of administrative organization. More plausibly, it should be seen as evidence of the opposition that was already building on Anjouan and Mohéli to a regime essentially based on Grande Comore.

The principal economic objectives of the regime were articulated in the five-year plan published in February 1978. High on the list of priorities were land reform and the achievement of self-sufficiency in food production. Vacant company land was distributed in small lots to landless peasants, but the regime did not appear to initiate any more radical agrarian reform and instead concentrated on instructing peasant farmers and improving peasant agriculture. A partly socialized agriculture was to be developed by state planning and investment, coordinating the work of private landowners. The value of export crops was to be maintained as far as possible, and therefore, a major redirection of agricultural effort was ruled out from the start.

Apart from the dramatic gestures like women burning their veils and the central government burning its archives, what is most striking about Ali Soilih's revolution is its extreme moderation. There was no systematic land confiscation or proscription of the feudal class of Arab notables. There was no repetition of the events in Zanzibar, and Marxist revolutionaries would scarcely have recognized Soilih as one of them. The objectives of the five-year plan were eminently sensible and could well have been acceptable to France or to either of the old aristocratic parties. Nevertheless, by the time the plan was published Ali Soilih's regime was wallowing, half-sunk by fast-encroaching economic chaos.

During 1976 and still more during 1977, the islands began to suffer from severe food shortages. The United Nations had to hurry a consignment of 2,500 tons of rice to the Comoros as early as December 1975, but this was only the equivalent of a three-month supply.[41] Early in 1976 the Comoro government had to go begging to other sources for aid to survive from month to month. More food aid was obtained from the Economic Development Fund, and the Arab League gave some financial assistance. Refugees from Madagascar and natural disasters in 1977 attracted further small amounts of emergency aid, but any long-term finance that would enable systematic development to take place was withheld because no administration existed to handle the funds. Soilih's internal budget had to plan for a reduction in expenditure of seven-eighths (87.5 percent), and in many parts of the archipelago all economic life, apart from the most basic growing of food, came to a halt. Exports could not be moved, and imports could not be paid for. What foreign currency was available paid for food imports or was earmarked hopefully for cement and farm machinery. In the moudiryias public works and school programs halted for lack of funds. The plans to resettle the refugees among the villages also came to nothing for lack of funds or any means of administering the scheme.[42]

Meanwhile, Soilih's political problems were mounting. The foreign press concentrated, perhaps unfairly but certainly not unexpectedly, on the activities of the young revolutionaries and their unauthorized activities in the countryside, bullying villagers and intimidating erstwhile notables. There was widespread condemnation of the *"gouvernement par lycéens."* Rumors were rife that the Comoros were to be annexed by Tanzania and absorbed into that state, which had taken over Zanzibar following a similar sort of revolution. These rumors discouraged external aid, but internal resistance was also growing. The regime had to face outbreaks of opposition on Anjouan and, more seriously, on Mohéli, where a major revolt took place among the peasantry, who had always been relatively free of feudal overlords, had never suffered acutely from land shortage, and who now feared the policies of the revolutionary government. For some weeks Mohéli remained virtually independent, and it was only in December 1977 that a detachment of the new army was landed to restore the government's authority. As food shortages increased, there were more clashes between the supporters of the regime, the *Moissi* gangs, and the army, on the one hand, and ordinary townsmen and villagers on the other. Fighting broke out at Iconi near the capital in March 1978.[43]

THE COMOROS SINCE SOILIH

On the night of May 12, 1978, a group of fifty French mercenaries landed on the beach of Itsandra, two miles from the capital, captured Ali Soilih, and overthrew his government. The leader of the mercenaries, Bob Denard, had already been involved in Comorian politics, having assisted in the coup that toppled Ahmed Abdullah in 1975 and paved the way for the rise of Soilih. He was a well-known figure in African politics and a veteran of coups and attempted coups in many countries.[44] Already in June 1978, the *Observer*'s correspondent in Paris, Robin Smyth, was reporting with remarkable prescience that the mercenaries' next target would be the Seychelles.[45] Denard easily took control of the Comoros and installed a provisional government led by former interior minister Said Atoumane. One of the earliest announcements of the new government declared, significantly, a restoration of "religious freedom," by which was meant the legalizing of the old religious ceremonies, particularly the *grand mariage.*

The ease with which a handful of mercenaries captured the Comoros and overthrew Soilih's regime was the result not so much of the president's unpopularity as of the complete lack of organization of his government. The coup was a humiliating example of the powerlessness of small states in the face of international banditry, and it was to encourage the belief that other regimes could be toppled as easily. The coup had apparently been financed by two of the richest Comorian exiles, Ahmed Abdullah, the former president, and Mohammed Ahmed, who allegedly raised some of the $2 million Denard demanded by mortgaging his Paris apartment. However, if the world only saw the involvement of

Die Stadt Aitanda Mdjini auf Angasija oder Groß-Komoro.

Itsandra (Grande Comore), 1864. (From Baron Claus von der Decken, *Reise in Ost-Afrika*, Leipzig, 1871.) It was on this beach that the mercenaries landed who overthrew Ali Soilih in 1978.

Denard and the two Comorian notables, there is little doubt that the French SDECE (secret service) was very active behind the scenes and that the French could have prevented the coup with ease had they so chosen.[46]

Ahmed Abdullah and Mohammed Ahmed returned to the Comoros on May 22, and within a week Soilih had been "shot while trying to escape." At this stage there were no further executions or purges, but many of those involved with the Soilih regime hastened to leave the country. Meanwhile, Abdullah and Ahmed installed themselves as joint presidents.

Such overt neo-colonialism was very unfavorably received in the world at large, and the OAU proceeded to expel the Comoros from its council of ministers, and Madagascar severed all links with the islands. France was, in fact, the only friend that the restored regime had, and even France proved somewhat wary of giving aid on the pre-1975 scale. The reason for French caution was the continued presence of Denard and his men in the islands. The mercenary commander showed every sign of wanting to establish himself permanently. He took a Muslim name and began attending mosques, and he and his friends enjoyed lucrative offices and appointments in the new government. In September it became known that there might be moves in the UN against the Comoros, and France began to put pressure on Denard to leave. In October the mercenaries made a well-publicized departure from the islands, and a French military mission officially took over the training of the defense forces.[47] This was not to be the end of Denard's association with the Comoros, but for the time being it was enough to appease international hostility.

Abdullah and his colleague set about drawing up yet another constitution. It was to have a federal structure, with each island having its own assembly, budget, and emergency executive powers. At the center, power lay emphatically with the president, and it surprised no one when in October Abdullah was once more installed as sole president. This constitution was almost certainly framed with the idea of facilitating the eventual reintegration of Mayotte, but it was a humiliating *volte face* for the man who had bravely challenged France in 1975 over the unity of the archipelago. The constitution was approved by the now traditional 99 percent "yes" vote after its clauses had been read out in nightly installments over the radio. In November the French finally signed a full military and economic accord, which among other things, allowed the French navy to make full use of the facilities of the islands.[48]

Having secured French backing once more, Abdullah moved to consolidate his position and eliminate his opponents. In December 1978 a compliant assembly banned all political parties for twelve years, effectively allowing Abdullah two full terms in office. Abdullah's power base remained the island of Anjouan, but he shrewdly distributed offices among notables from the other islands. His prime minister, for example, was Salim ben Ali from Grande Comore, and the president of the Supreme Court (established in April 1979) was Haribou Chebane, a judge from Mohéli. Early in 1979 a roundup of the supporters of the previous regime began. Four of Soilih's former ministers disappeared and allegedly were executed, and some 300 of his supporters were imprisoned without trial in Moroni.[49] Throughout the next two years there were sporadic rumors of further arrests, shootings, and disappearances until France demanded that prisoners be either released or brought to trial. In December 1980 some trials were held, but early in 1982 France again had to insist that political prisoners be either tried or released. In May 1982 the most important surviving member of Soilih's government, Mouzaoir Abdullah, was imprisoned for two years after allegedly trying to organize opposition in the islands.[50] Throughout this time Abdullah was protected by a presidential guard, which was still officered by Denard's men and was recruited and maintained quite separately from the other armed forces.

The new regime's most pressing need was to find sources of aid to rebuild the islands' economy and provide the administration with enough finance to survive from day to day. As before the revolution, the main investment and budgetary aid came from France, but a serious attempt was made to find other funds. The Soilih years may have borne some fruit here, for many of the friends that the islands had discovered during Soilih's administration proved willing to continue their support. Immediate budgetary aid came from the European Economic Community (EEC) and from France, and in 1979 a series of long-term development projects were announced, giving priority to road building, telecommunications, the building of the port of Mutsammudu, and the improving of international air links. Much of the aid for these projects came from Saudi Arabia, Kuwait, the Gulf Emirates, and the Arab Development Bank. Other aid was sought for agricultural projects, and a tentative five-year plan was published aiming at self-sufficiency in food—another echo of the thinking of the Soilih years. Loans were negotiated for fisheries, pest control, the improvement of copra-processing, etc.[51]

The economic recovery of the islands was, however, painfully slow. There was much inefficiency and corruption, and French technical assistance was not restored to pre-revolution levels. The president's enemies asserted that any wealth the islands possessed was being creamed off by Denard and his associates, who still visited the islands as "tourists," and who held important positions in the Comorian embassy in Paris and in the tourist industry. Indeed, it seems that Abdullah, Denard, and a Pakistani financier named Kalfane were operating something approaching a monopoly in the import and export trade of the islands.[52] Abdullah was prepared to condone openly Denard's continued association with the islands. In April 1981 he told Le Monde, "Pourquoi empêcherais-je Bob de venir ici, lui qui a libéré mon pays? Est-ce que je proteste contre la présence des Cubains à Madagascar?"[53]

In July 1980 Abdullah had to reinforce his regime with a cabinet change, but he retained the same prime minister. By this time political opposition once again was beginning to be heard, principally among Comorians in exile. The first group to raise its head appeared in 1979 under the acronym FNUC. (FNUC later became known as FNUK-UNIKOM—standing for Front National pour la Unification des Co-mores—Union Comorien.) It was made up of MOLINACO stalwarts and exiled members of Soilih's regime who had escaped to the safety of Kenya, where the movement was based and from which its propaganda was issued. FNUC concentrated on exposing Abdullah's repression and the active role that the mercenaries were still playing in the affairs of the archipelago.[54] Meanwhile, a Comorian youth organization (OJC—Organisation de Jeunesse Comorienne) with its base in Algiers began to try to organize Comorian workers in France, and ASEC, the students organization of the 1960s, revived and began to circulate a propaganda sheet, *La Voix du Peuple*, in the islands, filling the gap left by the demise of *Uhuru*.[55] At least one half-hearted attempt at a coup was made when Mouzaoir Abdullah returned secretly to the Comoros to organize op-position. The most significant development, however, occurred in July 1980 when the Comorian ambassador in Paris, Said Ali Kemal, resigned his post and formed the sinister-sounding Comité National de Salut Public, which demanded the resignation of Abdullah and closer ties with Madagascar, including the acceptance of the policy of an Indian Ocean Peace Zone. To attract domestic sympathy Kemal's group also demanded land reform. The emergence of Kemal's opposition group in Paris, clearly without active French disapproval, was a clear warning to Abdullah that France was prepared to see a credible alternative leadership take shape. In the short run the presence of Kemal in Paris was a device enabling the French to pressure Abdullah into reforming his government and mending his ways.[56] However, Kemal soon found himself courted by those whose interest in the Comoros was less than purely altruistic. Footloose mercenaries, shady international financiers and, allegedly, CIA agents worked on him and persuaded him during 1983 to add his name to a half-baked plan to seize the islands in a repetition of Denard's coup. In December 1983 some of the mercenaries, who had been arrested in Australia, went on trial, and the whole sordid affair received publicity enough to discredit Kemal. The failure of this coup, however, does not mean that the next one, or the one after the next, will not succeed. Until that time France appears more and more clearly as protector of Abdullah and, ultimately, as arbiter of his fate.

Abdullah, meanwhile, had been looking elsewhere for friends. As will be described more fully in Chapter 6, he sought to make the Comoros take their part in the evolving regional economic organizations and political alignments. He visited Kenya, the Gulf, and Libya in search of diplomatic support, and a Comorian delegate attended the non-aligned summit in 1981. None of this, however, freed him from French pressure, and by early 1982 a deteriorating local situation and the demands of his paymaster were forcing him to set his political house in order.

Early in 1982 discontent inside the country at the continued economic chaos was coming to a head. Civil servants were unpaid, and nurses and teachers went on strike. Still more serious was the fact that the army appeared to be the center of the dissidence. The army officers were well aware that they had not been entrusted with internal security and that Abdullah was protected by the presidential guard still under mercenary control. Therefore, agitation against Abdullah and the mercenaries had a natural appeal to the army. In January there had been severe food shortages once again, and the French told Abdullah that better economic management and an end to political repression were the conditions of further French aid. As a result, a tribunal was set up to try the remaining political prisoners, and in the search for greater economic efficiency Abdullah dismissed a third of the civil servants and agreed to the establishment of a state corporation to take over rice importing from his own firm. In February the prime minister, Salem ben Ali, was replaced by Ali Mroudjae, and a new political grouping, the Union Comorienne pour le Progrès, was formed to put up a list of candidates to support Abdullah in the coming elections. Held in March, the elections led to Abdullah's list winning all but one of the seats.[57]

Abdullah's restored regime, ever more precarious, living only from day to day, was also unsuccessful in solving the problem of Mayotte. In France right-wing politicians pressed the case of the Mahorais leaders for full departmental status, while resolutions at the United Nations and the OAU made it clear that international opinion would refuse to accept anything short of the reunification of the four islands. France adopted a masterly policy of compromise that kept all the options open. In 1979 it was decided that the status of *territoire* would be continued for another five years and would be followed by a referendum.[58] However, France was prepared to favor closer ties between the islands. Barriers were lowered, and free movement of people and goods was restored. The French even encouraged the formation of a political party, the Democratic Assembly, to rival Henry's Mouvement Mahorais, although this may have had something to do with the fact that Henry was offering strong support to the Gaullist cause in French elections. Abdullah, for his part, had made moves toward the reintegration of the islands. The 1978 constitution with its federal structure was clearly designed for the easy incorporation of Mayotte at some future date. The appointment of a Mahorais as finance minister was also significant. Beyond these gestures there was little that Moroni politicians could do. As Abdullah told *Le Monde*, "*L'Ile Comorienne de Mayotte est un sol comorien occupé par la France. Mais je ne vais tout de même pas lui déclarer la guerre.*"[59]

With Moroni so firmly tied to French apron strings, the only real obstacle to the reincorporation of Mayotte was to be found in French domestic politics where it was strongly opposed by the vociferous right wing Gaullist-Réunion lobby. The future reunification of the archipelago had come to depend on events in Paris or St. Denis and not on the actions or inactions of the Comorians themselves.

NOTES

1. Thierry Flobert, *Les Comores*, Travaux et mémoires de la faculté de Droit et de Science Politique d'Aix-Marseille No. 24 (Marseille: Aix-Marseille P.U., 1974), p. 335.

2. Jean Martin, "Les notions de clans, nobles et notables: leur impact dans la vie politique comorienne d'aujourd'hui," *L'Afrique et l'Asie*, vol. 81–82 (1968), p. 56.

3. C. Saint Alban, "Les partis politiques comoriens," *Revue française d'études politiques africaines*, October 1973, p. 78.

4. Ibid., p. 78.

5. André Bourde, "The Comoro Islands: Problems of a Microcosm," *The Journal of Modern African Studies* 3 (1965), p. 95; Jean Martin, "L'archipel des Comores," *Revue française d'études politiques africaines* 44 (1968), p. 23; K. Allaoui, "La France et les Comores de 1958 à nos jours à travers Le Monde, Le Figaro, La Dépêche du Midi et l'Humanité" (Masters thesis, Toulouse, 1976), pp. 37–40.

6. There were 71,099 electors on the roll of whom 65,920 voted and 63,899 voted *oui*. Figures in Allaoui, "La France et les Comores," p. 37. See note 30, this chapter, for reference to allegations of vote-rigging in Comorian elections.

7. Voting figures in the presidential elections were de Gaulle, 104,803 (99.42 percent), and Mitterrand, 601 (0.58 percent). Mitterrand claimed afterwards that *"même les morts"* had voted. Allaoui, "La France et les Comores," p. 42.

8. For Mayotte's separatist movement see H. Chagnoux and A. Haribou, *Les Comores* (Paris: Presses Universitaires de France, 1980), chapter entitled "L'Affaire de Mayotte"; Flobert, *Les Comores*, pp. 368–383.

9. Flobert, *Les Comores*, p. 373.

10. Ibid., pp. 198–199, 373.

11. Allaoui, "La France et les Comores," p. 47.

12. For MOLINACO see Saint Alban, "Les partis politiques comoriens," pp. 78–79; Martin, "L'archipel des Comores," pp. 34–35; Flobert, *Les Comores*, pp. 311–323.

13. Flobert, *Les Comores*, p. 321.

14. Allaoui, "La France et les Comores," p. 55. The two other important French TOMs were Tahiti and Djibouti.

15. Martin, "L'archipel des Comores," p. 33; Allaoui, "La France et les Comores," pp. 46–47.

16. Allaoui, "La France et les Comores, p. 51.

17. For PASOCO see Saint Alban, "Les partis politiques comoriens," pp. 86–87; Flobert, *Les Comores*, pp. 360–365; and most important of all, PASOCO's own cyclostyled journal *Uhuru*, published in Moroni.

18. Flobert, *Les Comores*, p. 365; John Ostheimer, "Political Development in the Comoros," *The African Review* 3 (1973), p. 501.

19. Anon., "Sous developpement et colonisation," *Uhuru* 13 (1973), p. 11.

20. Anon., "Quelques remarques sur le developpement," *Uhuru* 11 (1973), pp. 9–17.

21. For the two-year presidency of Said Ibrahim see Saint Alban, "Les partis politiques comoriens"; *Africa Contemporary Record,* vols. 3, 4, 5; and Ostheimer, "Political Development in the Comoros," Ostheimer's article, partly rewritten, appeared as "The Politics of Comorian Independence" in John Ostheimer, ed., *The Politics of the Western Indian Ocean Islands* (New York: Praeger, 1975), pp. 73–101.

22. "Comoro Islands," *Africa Contemporary Record* 4 (1971–1972), p. B388.

23. Allaoui, "La France et les Comores," p. 59.

24. Ibid., p. 59; L. Favoreu and J-C. Maestre, "L'accession des Comores à l'indépendence," *Annuaire des pays de l'Océan Indien* (1975), p. 18.

25. Ostheimer, "Political Development in the Comoros"; a political analysis by Philippe Decraene was published in *Le Monde,* 1 & 2 December 1972.

26. Author's observation made in 1973. Ahmed Abdullah was nicknamed *"président import-export"* according to Chagnoux and Haribou, *Les Comores,* p. 38.

27. Flobert, *Les Comores,* p. 377.

28. Ibid., p. 380.

29. Chagnoux and Haribou, *Les Comores,* p. 37.

30. For the controversy surrounding this vote, and by implication other Comorian elections, see "Mémoire des Députés du Mouvement Mahorais sur le Referendum du 22 décembre 1974 aux Comores," *Revue française d'études politiques africaines* 110 (1975), pp. 81–94.

31. "Comoro Islands," *Africa Contemporary Record* 8 (1975–1976), pp. B178–179; Favoreu and Maestre, "L'accession des Comores à l'indépendance," pp. 19–21.

32. For example, article entitled "Comoro Coup by Pro-Paris Group," *Guardian,* August 4, 1975.

33. Chagnoux and Haribou, *Les Comores,* p. 64; and J-C. Maestre, "Les Comores," *Annuaire des pays de l'Océan Indien* (1976), p. 343.

34. For an assessment of France's Indian Ocean strategy at this time see Michael Field, "Self-interest in the Comoros," *Daily Telegraph,* 29 October 1974; and "Comoro Islands," *Africa Contemporary Record* 8 (1975–1976), pp. B178–B185.

35. Chagnoux and Haribou, *Les Comores,* p. 69.

36. Ibid., p. 69.

37. The consequences of the break with France are spelled out in "Comoro Islands," *Africa Contemporary Record* 8 (1975–1976), p. B182; see also Maestre, "Les Comores."

38. "Comoro Islands," *Africa Contemporary Record* 10 (1977–1978), pp. B188–194.

39. Chagnoux and Haribou, *Les Comores,* pp. 75–76.

40. Ibid., p. 74.

41. *Africa Research Bulletin* 12 (1975), Economic, Financial and Technical series, December–January 1976.

42. "Comoro Islands," *Africa Contemporary Record* 8 (1975–1976), p. B184.

43. Chagnoux and Haribou, *Les Comores,* p. 81.

44. Numerous highly colored accounts of the Comoro coup were published at the time. See, for example, David Lamb, "Comoros: a Path to Democracy," *Los Angeles Times,* October 21, 1978; and Tony Avirgnan, "Col. Denard's Newly

Won Kingdom is no Island Paradise," *Guardian*, August 19, 1978. One of the more bizarre outcomes was that Denard was condemned to death in absentia by Benin. See *Africa Research Bulletin* 16 (1979), Political, Social and Cultural series, May 1979.

45. Robin Smyth, "Mercenary Hangs on to Power after Coup," *Observer*, June 25, 1978.

46. Smyth, in *Observer*.

47. Avirgnan, in *Guardian*; "Comoros Colonel forced out," despatch from Reuters in *Guardian*, September 27, 1978.

48. For the new constitution and the relationship with France after the fall of Soilih, see J. Latremolière, "La France et le nouvel état comorien," *Afrique Contemporaine*, November/December 1978, pp. 10–19.

49. "The Comoros," *Africa Contemporary Record* 12 (1979–1980), pp. B168–176.

50. *Africa Research Bulletin* (1982), Political, Social and Cultural series, May 1982.

51. For details of the aid and loans see *Africa Research Bulletin*, 1980, 1981, 1982.

52. "The Comoros," *Africa Contemporary Record* 13 (1980–1981), p. B146.

53. Interview given to Jean-Pierre Langellier of *Le Monde* and published April 25, 1981.

54. *Africa Research Bulletin* (1980), Political, Social and Cultural series, December 1979.

55. Langellier in *Le Monde*.

56. "The Comoros," *Africa Contemporary Record* 13 (1980–1981), p. B146.

57. For events in the Comoros from the beginning of 1982 onward see the weekly numbers of the *Indian Ocean Newsletter*.

58. Langellier in *Le Monde*; and Sadio Lamine Sow, "En Attendant Mayotte," *Jeune Afrique*, January 27, 1982.

59. Langellier in *Le Monde*.

4

Comorian Society

THE ETHNIC AND LINGUISTIC
COMPOSITION OF THE POPULATION

The early travelers who visited the Comoros spoke of three distinct sections of the population. At one end of the social spectrum were the rulers of the coastal towns, referred to as Arabs, who had light skin and wore "turkish" dress. They maintained a leisured and even cultivated existence in their stone-built houses—although not everyone gives as flattering a picture of this ruling class as does Sir William Jones in the 1780s who described meeting cultured Arab gentlemen with whom he could discuss music and manuscripts.[1]

At the opposite end of the spectrum were the slaves. Large numbers of slaves from Africa and Madagascar were brought to the islands for onward shipment, but some were always retained for domestic and agricultural service. Fryer wrote of the islands in 1672, "All four are colonies of the Moors or Arabians, or at least in subjection to them," and he goes on to mention that "their slaves have a dejected countenance . . . they sit on stones or low seats, their arms folded."

In between these two classes were the free inhabitants of the islands, descendants of migrants who had arrived over the centuries from Africa or Madagascar.[2]

These clear-cut social divisions were not really ethnically or linguistically distinct. François Pyrard, visiting the islands in 1601, wrote frankly, "They are a mixture of several races, as well from the coast of Ethiopia, Caffres and even Mulattoes as Arabs and Persians."[3] If some men who were Arabic-speaking and had Arabian features could be found among the ruling nobles, their numbers were few, for Muslim society was structured to bring about a mixture of races. The traders and dhow captains from East Africa, Arabia, and the Gulf had large households of slaves and a numerous progeny by their concubines. As a result, the predominant culture was one that mixed African, Arab, and Malgasy elements, the Arab influences being strongest in the coastal towns and among the ruling elites, the African traits strongest among

73

the peasant communities who lived inland. The whole formed what one writer has called *"un spectre de métissages."*[4]

In the nineteenth century the population changed rapidly. The Malagasy raids effected a great diminution of the population until considerable tracts of the archipelago were depopulated. Then, onto this vacant land came numbers of Merina and Sakalava, followers of the rival chiefs Ramanataka and Andriansouli. For a generation these Malagasy remained a recognizably distinct element in the life and politics of the islands. In addition, from the 1840s onward, there were large importations of slaves from Mozambique to provide labor for the plantations that sprang up on Mayotte, Anjouan, and Mohéli. This substantial immigration quickly reduced the descendants of the old population to a minority on both Mayotte and Mohéli and considerably altered the balance on Anjouan and Grande Comore as well.

For a generation at least, at the end of the nineteenth century, distinct ethnic groups could be readily distinguished among the island populations. Gevrey calculated that in 1870 10 percent of the people on Mohéli were of Arab descent, 20 percent were Merina from Madagascar, 40 percent were of African origin, and only 30 percent were descended from the original inhabitants of the islands, whom he called Antalotes and who were the result of earlier mixing of African and Malagasy settlers.[5] To this potpourri of peoples, groups that have arrived since the French protectorate was established should be added. The descendants of French creoles have continued to be a small but influential group on Mayotte, and Indian traders have established commercial networks on all four islands. There has also been some considerable movement of population between the overcrowded islands of Grande Comore and Anjouan and their two less densely populated neighbors. This movement was actively promoted under the presidency of Ahmed Abdullah and just as actively reversed when Mayotte broke away from the other three islands in 1975.

To a large extent these immigrant groups have come to accept the predominant Swahili culture of the islands. On Mohéli the descendants of the Merina have been Islamized and now speak *shimwali,* the local Swahili dialect. On Mayotte, integration has been less complete, and as late as 1975 the various groups lived in separate villages and retained their linguistic individuality. A Sakalava dialect, *kibushi,* was spoken in thirty-one out of seventy-two villages, and *shimaore*—a form of Swahili— was spoken in twenty-two. The remaining nineteen villages were occupied by recent immigrants from Grande Comore and Anjouan.[6] The latter villages were all situated inland and testified to the land hunger that led them to recolonize the wastes abandoned by the French *colons.* Although Islam is the religion of the overwhelming majority of Mahorais, there is a minority of Christians larger and considerably more vocal than exists on the other three islands. Mayotte separatist politicians have tended to emphasize, and probably exaggerate, the Christian and Malagasy cultural influences on Mayotte.

Anjouan has a somewhat different demographic history. There has been no appreciable immigration from Madagascar to Anjouan in modern times, but the nineteenth century witnessed the arrival of African slaves and *engagés* laborers on a large scale. The descendants of these laborers are still called *Makwa*—a name derived from the Macua-speaking peoples of northern Mozambique. The *Makwa* are now all Islamized and speak *shinzuani*—the island dialect.

Grande Comore was less affected than the other three islands by the population changes of the nineteenth century. A large part of the present population descends from elements long-established in the island, and this is reflected in the somewhat archaic structure of the *shingazidja* dialect.

The island dialects are sometimes loosely referred to as Swahili, and clearly they are closely related to that language, but Comorians are not readily intelligible to Swahili speakers of East Africa. Although distinct dialects are spoken on each of the islands, the Comoros do have a degree of linguistic and cultural homogeneity unusual in a modern African state. The descendants of the Arab notables are not a culturally distinct group, as were their counterparts in Zanzibar, and both they and the *Makwa* have adopted the language of the islands. The only considerable ethnic or linguistic minority are the *kibushi*-speaking population of Mayotte, but they are confined to a single island, and the overwhelming majority of them are Muslim and speak *shimaore* as well as their own tongue. Island separatism exists as an important political factor, but it is not exacerbated by ethnic, linguistic, and cultural divisions such as appear to dominate the politics of many African countries.

CLASS STRUCTURE

The class structure of the island community in part derives from ancient, traditional social divisions based on descent and in part reflects class structures emerging within the embryonic modern economy. Until a modern sector to the economy began to emerge in the 1960s, French rule had tended to support the feudal nature of society.

At the head of the social hierarchy was the narrow group of noble families who claimed descent from Arab or Persian forebears, and some of whom were accepted as *sharifs*—descendants of the Prophet. On Anjouan these nobles are collectively called the *gabila*.[7] They used to inhabit their own quarter in the towns of Moya, Wani, Domoni, and Mutsammudu, where they monopolized religious and political functions and where many of them also owned land. The nobles always married among themselves, at least as far as the *grand mariage* was concerned, but for secondary marriages the rules were not so strict. It is impossible to calculate the size of this social group, but on Anjouan it formed only a small part of the urban population, which itself is only 12 percent of the island's people. The nobles are an equally powerful group on

Brunnen und Bethaus auf Großkomoro.

A well and mosque on Grande Comore, 1864 (From Baron Claus von der Decken, *Reise in Ost-Afrika*, Leipzig, 1871)

Grande Comore, but they have largely disappeared from Mayotte and Mohéli, where the class structure signally lacks this traditional élite.

Many of the nobility identified closely with the French overrule. Some served with the French armed forces and became strongly Gaullist, while others received a French education and took an increasingly prominent part in the administration of the islands. The first two presidents of the Governing Council, Said Mohammed Cheik and Prince Said Ibrahim, were from the noble families of Grande Comore.

The group immediately below the nobility were the freemen (called *ongouana* on Grande Comore and *wamatsaha* on Anjouan).[8] They were either urban dwellers who adopted the life-style of the nobility and even intermarried with them, artisans, or simply peasants who had always been free.

Finally, there were the slaves (on Anjouan known as *wadzalyia* or *makwa*, and on Grande Comore as *watwana*). With the abolition of slavery the distinction between descendants of former slaves and former freemen has inevitably blurred and been largely superseded by new class divisions based on economic status. However, relics of the old social order can still be traced, for instance, in the case of fishermen whose profession is viewed as servile and who still frequently live in their own villages or in their own quarter of a town, sometimes even having their own mosques and headmen.

Traditional social divisions began to be radically transformed when the concession companies took over large parts of the two most populous islands—Anjouan and Grande Comore. Many peasants were then forced to work for the companies in return for being allowed to occupy and farm small plots of land. As the land companies slowly relinquished their holdings, the peasantry tended to remain the de facto owners. On land owned by nobles a system of sharecropping in which the peasant might have to hand over a third or more of his crop survived in many parts until the Soilih revolution. However, there was a gradual weakening of the position of the noble landowners as many peasants occupied their land as illegal squatters. The contrast with Mohéli and Mayotte is great. On these islands there was no entrenched noble class, and the French creole planters who dominated the islands in the early part of the twentieth century for the most part abandoned their land due to lack of labor and the collapse of the sugar industry. A free peasantry moved in to occupy the derelict estates, and immigrant farmers arrived from the other two islands.

The movement toward consolidating the position of a free peasantry has gained added impetus from the decline of the companies as primary producers of export crops. Much vanilla, ylang-ylang, and copra is now peasant-produced. On the other hand, rapid population growth is pauperizing many of the village communities as quickly as they can establish some degree of independence. On Mohéli and Mayotte the population pressure is less, and the comparative lack of land hunger makes the peasantry more independent. This has had some political significance in the evolution of Mayotte separatism and in Mohéli's resistance to Ali Soilih's revolutionary government.

The emergence of a modern sector in the economy in the 1960s coupled with rapid population growth is creating a new urban class structure. Through being incorporated in the French empire some Comorians obtained opportunities to travel abroad and receive a French education. Eventually, in 1959, a *lycée* was established in Moroni, and some Comorians who were educated enough to occupy professional and technical positions in their own administration began to receive appointments.[9] Although most of these new opportunities fell to members of the old noble class, an administrative bourgeoisie, drawing its members from a somewhat wider social background, also began to emerge.

French investment in the islands, little as it was, also encouraged the growth of an urban working class. Moroni in particular began to grow fast after the French moved their administrative headquarters there in 1964. In 1958 the town's population was about 3,297, but it had risen to 25,000 by the time of independence. The wage-earning section of the population grew, particularly in the fields of industrial workshops, transport, and construction, but by 1972 still only 7.6 percent of the island's population was wage-earning.[10]

The emergence of Moroni as a modern town is important in a way that has little to do with numbers. In this town are concentrated the archipelago's communications and government offices, there is the *lycée*, and a proletariat is emerging. This situation enables political consciousness to be stimulated in a way impossible in the older towns, and modern political life becomes a possibility.

It is important not to exaggerate the extent to which the old social divisions have given way to the new. Although by the time of independence a modern class structure had begun to emerge, its influence had been diluted by the numbers of foreigners who still serviced the technical and professional sides of government. Some 800 French expatriates ran the islands' services together with at least 300 Malagasy who occupied many of the technical posts at a lower level. The Indian community continued to dominate retailing, so access to the modern sector of the economy for native Comorians was somewhat limited.[11]

The class structure of the islands was complicated still further by emigration and the existence of large communities of Comorians overseas.[12] Emigration to Madagascar began as a movement of plantation workers in 1912, and by 1934 there were about 14,000 Comorians on the island. The number rose steeply after World War II, with the greatest number of people leaving the overpopulated villages on Grande Comore. A peak was probably reached in 1974, when there were some 60,000 Comorians on Madagascar. Of course, many of these had been born abroad, but probably a majority retained links with the island, sent remittances home, and returned there after a time. A similar emigration took place to East Africa; the historic ties with the Swahili cities had led to the existence of Comorian communities from early times. Some of these emigrants fought in the British armed forces, joined the colonial police, and became anglicized. Others moved on in search of work within British Africa, and some Comorians were even to be found working in the mines in South Africa. At the time of independence there may have been 40,000–50,000 Comorians in Africa, most of them living in Tanzania.

In 1975 Comorians living abroad comprised about a quarter of the Comorian people as a whole. The emigration led to a chronic imbalance between the sexes, as it was largely young men who left to work and to earn the money with which to make a traditional marriage. An estimate for 1976 suggested that women exceeded men in the population for every age group from twenty-five years of age onward.[13] For the young men who went abroad emigration was of particular relevance to their social aspirations. Without a period of working abroad it would be impossible for most of them to earn the very considerable sums (estimated at seven-years' income or more) needed to make a traditional marriage, without which they would not be accepted as a fully participating member of their home village or community. Emigration was thus a powerful factor supporting the continuation of the traditional social divisions based on religion, age-group, family connections, and the performance of traditional social functions. At the same time emigration meant that many Comorians expanded their horizons, their experience of the world, and the range of their skills. It meant that a greater proportion of the island's men participated in some sector of a modern economy than if they had stayed at home.

RELIGION

It is no coincidence that in seeking a total transformation of Comorian society Ali Soilih should have attacked the power of the dominant religious elite. In 1975 the greatest single influence in the life of a Comorian, whether from a noble family or from a poor peasant household, was religion. In 1615 Sir Thomas Roe's chaplain had written of the Comorians, "all the people are strict Mahometans, observing much of the ould Lawe . . . they are very jealous to let their women and their Moschees be seen."[14] Much the same could have been said of the islands 350 years later, and there are few countries in the world where Islam holds such sway and has been so little changed by the forces of modernism.[15]

Apart from some Indian Ismaelis, who have their own mosque in Moroni, all Muslims in the Comoros observe the Shaafi rite. Until the coming of the French, Islam was the vehicle for culture and communication. The members of the ruling class spoke and wrote Arabic, made pilgrimages to Mecca, and had family and commercial ties with other Muslim communities on the shores of the Indian Ocean. In their turn the islands were visited by important Muslim teachers and through the founding of brotherhoods kept in touch with the main developments of Islamic thought. Two brotherhoods are particularly active—the Rifay and the Shadilyya—the latter founded by Sheikh Sayyid Muhammad ibn Shaikh, who lived in the Comoros and died there around 1920.

In the towns Islamic observance is all pervasive, though French influence among the young may be weakening Islam's hold in a perceptible way. On Grande Comore and Anjouan each of the main towns have upward of thirty mosques and the smaller ones from ten to twenty. These range from imposing palaces, like the great Friday Mosque on the waterfront at Moroni, to little stone huts with tin roofs and palm mats, lacking windows or doors. A mosque is seldom pulled down, and when the community decides to build a bigger and better one, a new site is chosen and the old mosque is simply left to decay in neglect.

There are several reasons for the large number of mosques: Some have in them the tombs of venerated holy men; some are associated with a prominent local figure or ruling family of pre-French days; some mosques serve a particular quarter of the town; some are especially frequented by the young; and some mosques are even associated with the main political parties. On Grande Comore women do not enter the main mosques but either have a hut of their own for prayers or use the seashore. On Anjouan the women are allowed into the mosques but must sit behind screens or curtains. In the Comoros, Islam is particularly associated with the sea. Mosques are frequently sited looking out over the sea, as at Moroni or Fumboni on Grande Comore, and it is quite common to come across small mosques in isolated places on the seashore itself. Cemeteries were also placed near the sea at one time, and the coast north of Moroni still has two very prominent pillar-tombs—so prominent, in fact, that one is tempted to believe that these pillars had some navigational as well as commemorative purpose.

Once a week the male population gathers in the Friday Mosque, but on other days regular prayers are held in the other mosques of the town. In the smaller mosques the call to prayer is made from the doorway; larger mosques have a stairway leading to the roof or to a minaret, and it is not uncommon now for the *muezzin*'s call to be amplified or even recorded. When not in use for prayers a mosque will be a meeting place and almost a club for its habitués. Old men sit in the shade of the mosque verandah and talk, or they sleep inside in the cool. Beggars and the destitute come to a mosque for alms or shelter.

It would be quite wrong to suggest that strict Islamic practice is confined to the ruling classes of Grande Comore and Anjouan, but it is certainly true that mosques and mosque observance is much less evident in rural areas and on the islands of Mohéli and Mayotte. This is probably due, in part, to the fact that agricultural labor does not leave enough leisure time for sitting in mosques and in part to the fact that the old ruling class, the status of which is so closely tied up with religious observance, has almost disappeared from the two smaller islands and is usually not resident in the country areas.

The Muslim year is divided by certain well-established festivals: the *maulid* early in August, which commemorates the birth of the Prophet; *ramadan;* and the *miradji,* which celebrates the ascension of the Prophet into heaven. The *maulid* is followed by thirty days of dances, communal meals, and prayers. In the country the planting season is reckoned from the *maulid*—the first crop, bananas, is put in thirty days later. The most popular season for celebrating the *grand mariage* also occurs after the *maulid,* although this seems to have as much to do with the fine weather at that time of year and with the fact that the schools are on holiday as it does with religious considerations.

Ramadan dates from the first sighting of the new moon in September and lasts a month. There is a rather curious description of the celebration of *ramadan* given by a British sailor who visited Anjouan in 1821:

> As we landed, the lower rim of the sun was just kissing the horizon; hundreds of the natives were assembled on the sea-shore, watching its declining rays, and when the glorious orb had sunk beneath the waves, they laid themselves prostrate on the ground with their faces turned towards the spot where it had so majestically disappeared. . . . Presently they uttered a loud prayer and rose upon their knees; then standing upright, crossed themselves, and bowing, as it were, to the sunken luminary they began to hello and dance about like mad people. After the ceremony they had recourse to their chunam, bettle nut, tobacco etc. and fully made up, from the quantities which they crammed into their mouths, for having fasted all day. They then separated to their homes, in order to break their fast.[16]

No one visiting the islands today will see quite such a spectacular display of communal worship.

In addition to the main festivals of the Islamic year there is the annual pilgrimage to Mecca, which is made by a small number of people from each island. This observance still carries with it prestige and the right to be designated *al hadj,* and it is performed by perhaps 150 Comorians a year. Returning pilgrims bring with them colored prints of Medina and Mecca or little plastic souvenirs of the *kaaba.* However, the high cost of the pilgrimage, as high as the cost of the *grand mariage,* places it beyond the reach of all but a few, and it is probably true that today it is no longer the highest aspiration of all Muslims and is considered by many to be a waste of time and money.

Islamic observance still marks the passage through life of most Comorians, and the richer the family the more elaborate the celebrations. In the first five years of his life a boy undergoes the ceremonial cutting of the hair and circumcision. These ceremonies are limited to the family, but they are seldom observed without feasts and music. At about the age of seven, children of both sexes start to attend the *Koran* school.

In rural areas going to school may involve living away from home and working for the teacher on his land. At about ten years of age, if a child is fortunate, he or she begins to attend the French school and starts the slow climb up the ladder of Western education. At fifteen the onset of puberty is celebrated with more festivities (*m'tsamio*), and a boy may then be expected to herd cattle, seek work in the town or village, and set up a house of his own with his friends. The peer group is, indeed, very important, and arrangements exist for members of a peer group (*hirimu*) to save and to own property in common. Between eighteen and twenty a man can expect to marry for the first time and will travel either to a town or abroad in search of work.[17]

Descent, kinship, and inheritance are complex matters in the Comoros. Although a man inherits social status from his father and, in the case of the noble families, may be proud to identify with his father's lineage, for many practical purposes it is the matrilineage that is most important. Landed property, for example, belongs to the matrilineage and is administered on its behalf by the eldest sister. Property can be bought or inherited from the father, and there is an arrangement, called *maniahuli*, whereby brothers and sisters may hold such property in common. Eventually, however, this property is absorbed into the property of the matrilineage. Women also own house property, and on marriage, a man goes to live in his wife's house. Yet this importance of women in the field of land and property ownership has not prevented Islamic custom from establishing politics and social influence as mostly a male preserve. Clearly, as one writer has put it, "an underlying matrilineal organisation struggles with the strong emphasis on patrifiliation imported with Islam."[18]

Orthodox observance of all the feasts and obligations, together with a thorough knowledge of Islamic teaching and law, is probably the preserve only of wealthy urban families. Elsewhere Islamic observance is more or less diluted by poverty and the work patterns of the rural community. Both town and country, however, accord an important role to the *mwalimu*. The Muslim *mu'allim*, which the Swahili render *mwalimu*, are astrologers, medicine men, and in general, people who are learned in the use of sacred texts and sacred knowledge.[19] The *mwalimu* is consulted to discover which days will be propitious for the holding of ceremonies or feasts; he is consulted to see whether a proposed marriage will be favorable—and on this occasion his function comes close to being that of a matchmaker; he writes out sacred texts to be worn as amulets, and most children carry such little sachets of sewn goatskin around their necks; and he also is consulted in cases of illness. There is a quaint description of a *mwalimu* at work in Fryer's seventeenth-century account of the islanders: "However they are not so abject but that they have the use of letters and some science in astrology by what I can testify . . . I saw a man writing with a pen made of a cane in the bottom of a bowl besmeared with black."[20] The bowl would then be filled with water, and when the writing had dissolved, the magic potion would be drunk by the sick person.

In certain circumstances Islam may be a radical, puritanical, or revolutionary force, but in the Comoros its chief influence has been to support and justify a conservative social order. The old structure of ruling families was theocratic—the sultans were regarded as leaders of the religious community as well as heads of the secular state. In addition many of the leading families claimed to be *sharifs*, a claim that still carries prestige as can be seen at Wani, where the *sharif* families have a separate cemetery. More important, perhaps, than the conservatism of social class is the deeper conservatism enshrined in the law. The *qadis* still administer what is essentially traditional Islamic justice, and this has very conservative implications, particularly in the field of personal law and marriage.

MARRIAGE AND THE STATUS OF WOMEN

Until the time of Ali Soilih's revolutionary government, all Comorian men hoped to realize their social ambitions through contracting the *grand mariage* and thereby to become accepted fully into the adult society of the mosque and village councils.[21] Most women also expected to contract a traditional Muslim marriage and so gain the respect of their family and the community through their jewels, dress, and property. There are, however, three different sorts of marriage in Comorian society. The first is a simple contract made between a man and a woman before a *qadi*. It is a private marriage that does not involve expense, and it will be the first kind of marriage that a man will contract. Then there is the marriage that is solemnized with religious observances and mosque prayers. Finally, there is the *grand mariage*—a carefully planned union between families that is accompanied by lavish expenditure, public ceremonies, and exchanges of property.

It is still quite common for wealthy Comorian men to marry two or three wives, and this custom shows little sign of disappearing under the influence of Western education, for it is the wealthy, French-speaking ruling elite who can best afford to indulge in it. A survey carried out in 1958 showed that of the married men in Mutsammudu, the capital of Anjouan, 68 percent had one wife, 26 percent had two, 5 percent had three, and 1 percent had the four wives allowed by Islamic law. The rate of polygamy in the Comoros is generally high for a Muslim country.[22]

Polygamy can, indeed, only be practiced by the well-off. Each wife has her own house and establishment, often in a different part of the island or even on a different island altogether from other wives. This can cause problems for the husband, for Comorian law explicitly states that "a man must live with his wife. If he has more than one he must visit each in turn in such a way that none of them can claim to be neglected."[23] Nevertheless, it is not uncommon for a woman to be left alone at home while her husband goes to study in France or to work in Madagascar or Tanzania. For men, divorce is easy to obtain, and a woman's position in the marriage is far from secure—her main security, in fact, being her possession of the family home, which she retains after a divorce.

A married woman of the wealthy urban classes used to be expected to live a life of complete seclusion:

> After marriage, the wives are not allowed to see any of the male branches of their family but their fathers, and they are kept closely confined, that they are never allowed to walk out till night, and then only in their walled gardens or on the roofs of their houses. . . . At these times they are accompanied by their husbands and female slaves.[24]

This was the position of women as viewed by a British naval officer in 1821. Complete seclusion of this kind is now a thing of the past, although it is still quite common to see old houses with carved harem shutters on the upper stories, and until Soilih's revolution, quite a number of women on Grande Comore still wore black robes covering their heads and faces. It is still unusual for women to eat with men—particularly if guests have been invited.

Although women have been excluded in this way from male society and from public affairs, they still retain considerable influence in the community. Houses and landed property belong to the matrilineage and are administered by the eldest sister. A woman's children can, in a manner typical of the matrilineal societies of Africa, expect support and protection from their uncles as well as their father, and the uncles will also contribute toward marriage costs. On Mayotte, where the dominance of Muslim patriarchal values has weakened, this underlying strength in the position of women has come to the surface in the influential women's political organization on the island.

There is considerable difference in the status of women between the social classes and from island to island. Wives of the poorer members of society not only freely appear in the streets but also run market stalls and work in the fields. On Mohéli and Mayotte where the ruling Islamic elite is less dominant, the seclusion of women is not so strictly practiced. The commonest form of dress for women of all ages and all classes is the *chirumani*, a length of printed cotton wound around the body, and which can be brought over the head and face with a single movement of the hand. This marvelous garment can be highly decorative through the rich variety of prints that are now available and can be an expression of regional and class variations. On Mayotte the *chirumani* can be seen in its full wealth of color, but on Anjouan all women wear prints of the same dark claret color although of different designs. This garment can express traditional modesty or it can be the instrument of flirtation when worn by girls from the *lycée* promenading on the streets

Women wearing the *chirumani* in a Moroni market

of Moroni. It can even be combined with high fashion, and it is not unknown for this traditional form of dress to cover, though not entirely to hide, a trouser-suit or even a mini-skirt.

LE GRAND MARIAGE (NDOLA NKUU)

Before the eruptions of Soilih's revolutionary government the ceremonies associated with the *grand mariage* were the most striking public manifestations of Comorian communal and religious life.[25] The *grand mariage* has always been much more than just a marriage. It has been a major occasion for a family to make a statement about its social position, its aspirations, and its influence in the community. The public display associated with the marriage can be so lavish and economically so crippling for those involved that it should be viewed as a sort of Islamic version of the American Indian potlatch.

The ceremonial steps by which the marriage is completed last for many months and involve the families of the bride and bridegroom, their peer groups, and the wider community of town or village. The process begins when the family of a young man begins to make inquiries about a suitable bride. The girl's family is approached, and then a *mwalimu*, who is supposed to cast a horoscope for the pair to see if the signs are propitious, is contacted. It may be assumed, however, that he also makes inquiries into the standing of the families and the general suitability of the match.

Once the *mwalimu* has declared the match to be suitable, an exchange of presents (*mwafaka*) takes place, and the way is open for the formal betrothal. A special prayer (*badri*) is said for the protection of the couple, and this is accompanied by a feast offered by the bridegroom to his father-in-law's friends. This second ceremony involves the whole community in a dance through the streets carrying candles and chanting. In this, as in all other public ceremonies, a great deal of money is spent to assert the honor and status of those involved. The third ceremony involves handing over the brideprice—*zindrou* on Grande Comore, *mahari* on Anjouan. This is a substantial sum of money paid by the groom to the father of the bride that is supposed to contribute to the building of the house that will be the main present from the bride to her husband when the marriage is solemnized. At one time there was also an important ceremony, *karamou*, in which seven head of cattle were slaughtered in a kind of rodeo, the meat being distributed by the father of the bride to his own age-group and to the bridegroom.

The marriage itself may take place at any time after the betrothal, which may mean anything from one to five or ten years. The main ceremonies of the marriage take place over three days, starting on a Friday with a ceremonial meal in the new house, to which all the groom's age-group are invited. This meal is followed by a great public dance—the *toirab*—which is today the central event of the marriage. The dance lasts all night, and at dawn the jewels that the bridegroom offers to his bride in compensation for the loss of her virginity are publicly displayed. On Saturday there is the formal presentation of a large cake to the bridegroom by the bride's family, and in the evening there are more public dances, including a candle-lit procession.

On Sunday the husband is formally led to his bride, and in former times, this might be the first occasion on which he would see her. The nuptials last for nine days, during which time the husband does not leave his wife's house and the couple are attended by the husband's friends and by female servants of the bride. At the end of the nine days the bridegroom has to make a wide distribution of presents to his bride, her family, and those who have officiated at the wedding. The final public ceremony is the famous sword dance—the *tari landzia*—which takes place in the main street a week after the marriage and which is another important occasion when the men of the community assert their position in the local hierarchy.

The expenses of the *grand mariage* can be considerable even by the standards of the rich Western world. A bridegroom who wishes to acquit himself well in the *grand mariage* has to pay a brideprice and supply jewels and gold ornaments that alone, one writer estimated in 1974, can come to £1,000.[26] In addition he will have to pay for a number of feasts and communal meals in which meat, an expensive and prestigious item, has to be offered; for presents for the bride's family; for the cost of musicians; and for furniture and personal gifts for the bride herself.

The cost is scarcely less expensive for the bride's family. The obligation to provide a house may be burdensome, and frequently new houses cannot be completed and are left half-built. Mutsammudu before the revolution had a whole suburb of half-finished houses, making it look like the aftermath of a blitz. Frequently the bride's parents present their own house, and they look for somewhere smaller to live.

The overall cost of a marriage is impossible to calculate, but some believe that it runs to the equivalent of six or seven times a person's annual income. It is not surprising, therefore, that a family may take ten or fifteen years to accumulate enough cash to acquit themselves well in the *grand mariage* and that a large and well-organized wedding can bankrupt even the wealthiest family. Frequently only one son in a family will be able to marry in this way—the other members all working and saving for the big event. Comorians devote so much of their savings to paying for marriage that there is very little accumulated capital available for economic enterprises, and the underdevelopment of the islands is due in large part to the competitiveness of the *grand mariage*.

The *grand mariage* is an occasion when the poor majority of the population is forced into the role of being admiring spectators, the center of the stage held by those with political position and social prestige who indulge in an uninhibited display of their supposed wealth. At the same time, in pre-Soilih days, Comorians found in the ceremonies of the *grand mariage* the fullest expression of their culture; and artists, craftsmen, and musicians made it the greatest occasion for the display of their skills. The gold- and silversmiths of the islands live chiefly from their commissions to supply jewelry for the weddings. Made principally of gold, the jewelry traditionally includes a necklace of heavy and elaborate design, ear and finger rings, gold-decorated haircombs, bracelets, a chain for the forehead, and nose studs. Today a gold watch is usually also part of the regalia. These jewels are still worn by women at public functions, and some will wear them whenever they go out of the house. It is not uncommon to ride in a ferry from Pamanzi to the *grand terre* of Mayotte and be surrounded with women wearing hundreds of pounds worth of gold.

The massive cost of the *grand mariage* has inexorably led to its gradual simplification, and the *toirab*, the great public dance, has become the central feature of the display. Most old Comorian towns have a main square, sometimes with stone benches arranged around the edge, and are approached through elaborately decorated, Islamic-style gateways. Here the dances are held, with favored guests seated on chairs, older men placed around the square, and women and children climbing onto the roofs and crowding the windows. The musicians have expensive modern amplifying equipment and also play violins, guitars, African drums, and lutes. The music has strong elements of Arab rhythm, and many of the refrains are well known to the crowd, which joins in the singing. The music lasts for nine or ten hours, one singer after another holding the stage, and band succeeding band every two hours or so.

No sooner are the notables assembled than the dancing begins. First one man, then another, takes the aisle between the chairs and advances, smirking, pirouetting, turning, and waving in the air banknotes of greater or lesser denominations. As he reaches the band, he throws the money onto the stage or thrusts it into the pocket or down the shirtfront of one of the musicians. He then waltzes back to his seat. As the evening goes on, the public comes forward in increasing numbers, waving their money and carpeting the stage with banknotes. Every so often these are collected into suitcases and taken away into the wings. The sums collected go toward community projects and are an honor paid to the bridegroom, an appreciation of the band's performance, and a display of the giver's personal wealth and generosity.

Modern ways have invaded the *toirab*. Smart suits and red fezes are replacing the traditional white Muslim robes and caps, and electric guitars are ousting the older and more traditional instruments. It is not uncommon now to see a Comorian with modern ideas dancing forward waving not a banknote, but a checkbook and fountain pen.

The *grand mariage* was still common up to the eve of the Soilih coup. Some of the younger generation were critical of it, but few had rejected it and all its implications openly. Many radicals, however, had already identified it as the chief support of a social order based on hierarchy and the ownership of property and saw it as one of the principal reasons for the backwardness of the country's economy. As the socialist party, PASOCO, wrote in its little cyclostyled journal *Uhuru* in 1973:

> To refute this argument certain people may say that no one is obliged to contract the *grand mariage* if he is not able to. But this is to forget that in a society which functions on the principle of honour and hierarchy, the individual who does not accept the principle feels himself to be a stranger in one way or another.

Or again,

> what is the basis of the *grand mariage* but the seeking of honour which manifests itself in having an undisputed say in the religious, judicial, economic and other affairs of the village.[27]

Banning these marriage ceremonies certainly was a high priority for Ali Soilih's government in its efforts to regenerate the islands' economy and open up society, and it is probable that few people are really keen to see it reinstated in its full splendor. It is only sad that with the disappearance of the *grand mariage* may disappear many picturesque features of Comorian life and the occasion when traditional songs and dances are given their main opportunity to flourish.

NON-ISLAMIC SURVIVALS

It is easy, in stressing the Islamic nature of Comorian society, to forget the other influences from Africa and Madagascar that have been at work. Many customs and beliefs of non-Islamic origin survive to make the way of life in Comorian villages an impressive witness to the success with which Islam grafts itself onto existing cultures, assimilating without entirely obliterating them.

At one time spirit possession was common in parts of the Comoros.[28] Individuals, usually women, would be possessed by the spirits of chiefs or ancestors and, when in the state of possession (*tromba*), would act as oracles or prophets. The possessed would be given presents, and sometimes the whole community would take part in dances to stimulate possession. The *mwalimu* is also thought of as a mediator between the spirits and people in this world, but he does not have to be in a state of possession and can wield a more consistent, continuous, and rational authority. Spirit possession of this kind is common both in east-central Africa and on Madagascar (*tromba* is a term also used by the Sakalava), and it is, perhaps, more than a coincidence that some of the Shona mediums are referred to as *Mlimu*—a name that may have a distant Arabic origin.

Until the early part of this century witchcraft was common in the islands, and cattle and goats (and allegedly humans as well at one time) were sacrificed to procure the intervention of evil spirits to someone's detriment. For example, attempts were made to bring evil on the first French settlers on Mohéli by obtaining the intervention of a sorcerer from Grande Comore. The evil spirits did not always require the death of the cattle, and sometimes a cow dedicated to the spirits was allowed to roam free and unmolested until the spirit decided to end the cow's life. The Hindu overtones of the practice are obvious.

Lake Dzialandze on Anjouan was for long thought to be the special abode of the spirits. In 1636 Peter Mundy was told,

> There is by report aloft among the toppes of the Hilles a large and Deepe tancke or lake, of which are told strange stories (beeleeved by some), as that it hath no bottome, butt thatt there is a passage From thence into the Sea and thatt certaine blacke Fowle ly hovering over it and take any sticks or leaves thatt should Fall into it to Defile it: superstitiously great holinesse and respect to the said pond, The Chiefe of the Iland resorting thither once a yeare to wash themselves and to performe certaine ceremonies to it. They holde allsoe if any straunger should Chance to wash in it, it would bee polluted and thatt then the Iland would suffer Calamities as sicknesse, Dearth, Death, Foule wether.[29]

In more recent times the summoning of evil spirits (*sadaka*) often took place near the lake's shore.

Other ceremonies and rituals that clearly belong to a non-Islamic culture, particularly those observances associated with the paying of respect to the ancestors, are still performed in parts of the islands. The *koma* is a sacrifice and public festival irregularly carried out in the town of Wani on Anjouan. It is associated with two families—Beja and Combo—who claim descent from pre-Shirazi chiefs of the island, and it is also connected with the beginning of the year and the planting season. Islam has secured a toehold in this ceremony, which starts with possession and consultation of the spirits (*djinns*). These spirits reveal the day when the festival should be held. When the day arrives, a bull is chosen of the requisite red-brown color, the inhabitants of neighboring towns are invited, and the bull is ceremonially trussed and killed with its head pointing toward Mecca. As the animal is cut up and cooked, the men of the two families take part in a ball game in which three balls are batted about a marked ground. The balls carry with them prosperity for the coming harvest, and the part of the island toward which they are batted prospers accordingly.

Other ceremonies connected with the beginning of the agricultural year take place in remoter rural areas of the archipelago where Islamic influence is less strong. On Anjouan, for example, processions set out from the villages led by a figure clad in green who wields a large stick to stir up the dancers. The procession moves from village to village, stopping in one for the night, and the next day moving on until a place is reached near the sea, where a bull is slaughtered. A public dance ensues in which, it is alleged, all restraints between the sexes are dispensed with. The entrails of the animal are then thrown into the sea. It has been suggested that this ceremony derives from some cult in which the spirits of the sea have to be propitiated. The entrails of the bull are offered in order to preserve the lives of fishermen whom the spirits might otherwise have taken.

The preoccupation with cattle in all these ceremonies clearly looks to the great cattle cultures of Madagascar and the central African plateau. Cattle also used to play a large role in the *grand mariage* and still do have a part in public recreation. Bullfights still take place in some towns, where a bull post for tethering the animal can be seen in the main square. Similar bullfights used to take place on Pemba Island near Zanzibar.

WESTERNIZATION

This traditional society of nobles and peasants, in which the social order was largely structured and upheld by religious institutions, was directly and radically attacked by the revolutionary government of Ali Soilih. The radical phase of his government lasted from the middle of 1976 until his overthrow in the middle of 1978. Soilih's aim was to put an end to colonial dependence and centralization and to restructure society on the basis of village or district communes that were to be free from religious influence. The *grand mariage* was forbidden, and the emancipation of women decreed. Groups of female supporters of the regime gave up the *chirumani* and joined the armed forces and the new administration. At the same time French technical personnel were relieved of their posts, the whole central bureaucracy was closed down, and the archives were burnt. Encouragement was given to what was hoped would prove to be a new class, the young who had received some Western education and who had not had to gain status through the *grand mariage*.

Yet it is clear that such a radical program, even if it had been granted a period longer than two years for its realization, could make little progress while the economy remained so backward and while the vast majority of the population still accepted and lived by the old ideologies. It is relevant to ask, therefore, to what extent Westernization had taken root in the islands by 1975 and to what extent the grip of the hierarchical Islamic culture had been loosened.

Until World War II the French did not actively pursue a policy of assimilation and did little to interfere with traditional ways in education, medical care, and technology. Some schools were founded in the islands, but at the outbreak of the war there were scarcely a thousand pupils, representing 3 percent of the school-age group. By 1953 the number of students had risen to 10.8 percent and by 1969 to 20 percent. At the time of independence in 1975 perhaps 41 percent of the school-age group attended some form of French school, but only 8 percent went on to any kind of secondary education. The islands had five *collèges* (secondary schools) but only one *lycée*, at Moroni. Of the 2,174 pupils in secondary education half were attending the *lycée*. About 23 percent of those at secondary school were girls.[30] Other Comorians, though it is impossible to say how many, attended schools abroad, and all higher education had to be pursued in France. Technical education was virtually nonexistent in 1975, with only one technical school and one other school connected with the administration. In addition, there were one or two private establishments run by missions or other organizations, chiefly catering to the children of the well-off.

The *lycée* was founded in 1959, and it is only since then that an appreciable number of Comorians have obtained Western education. Their numbers are still small, for there has been a natural tendency for qualified Comorians to seek employment abroad and not return home to the poverty and lack of prospects in the islands. The vast majority of the population, in contrast, remains illiterate and ignorant even of the French language. It is estimated, for example, that on Mayotte only 5 percent of the population knew French when the referendum was held to determine whether the island should remain united to France. Moreover, such educational facilities that do exist are very poor in quality. A school was sometimes just a bare building lacking furniture, books, and frequently, a teacher. Nor was the education offered geared to local needs; students followed the French curriculum. Ali Soilih made a massive attack on educational backwardness and alleged that he raised the number of schools from 366 to 1,300 in two years. As with other matters, however, he fell from power before much could be realized permanently.

A similar picture can be painted of the provision of medical care at the time of independence. Because of the lack of adequate clean water-supplies, water-borne diseases, such as elephantiasis, malaria, and cholera, remained common. There was a serious outbreak of cholera on Grande Comore in 1975.[31] Apart from a WHO team working in the field of public health, there were few medical facilities. The French had built two main hospitals in Moroni and Mutsammudu with about 400 beds between them. There were a further seven small hospitals with a total of 200 beds that were able to offer limited maternity services and a clinic but little else. Even these facilities sometimes did not operate for lack of staff. In 1974 it was estimated that there was only 1 doctor to every 15,000 persons.[32] A bad situation became suddenly worse when the French withdrew most of their technical staff following the declaration of the islands' independence, and Mohéli, the island most affected, was left without a single doctor.

As already indicated, fewer than 10 percent of the active population were wage earners in the early 1970s—less then 5 percent of the population as a whole. Even these received wages so low that most were forced to supplement them with subsistence farming. Levels of consumption reflected levels of income and so helped to insulate the population from Western culture. Few of the islanders purchased consumer goods beyond oil lamps, tinned food, and cotton cloth. A few people owned radios, and there was a broadcasting station, but there were no newspapers and not even one printing press in the islands at the time of independence. Not only were telephones and electricity absent from all but the major administrative centers, but there were no bus services, and communications depended on a very irregular lorry and taxi service. In contrast to this, large sums of money (relative to the islanders' incomes, very large sums indeed) were expended on musical instruments and amplifying equipment. The rivalry of Comorian bands was proverbial, and the frequent open-air concerts and the opportunities provided by the *grand mariage* made music a potentially lucrative occupation for talented young men. The music itself seemed to derive as much from the beat of Liverpool and New Orleans as from Comorian tradition.

Among the elite families who held jobs in the French administration or who became members of the Council, other forms of Westernization were to be seen. Members of this class owned cars, wore smart lounge-suits and drank whiskey. For them the centers of Comorian life tended to be the bars of hotels where visiting French officials and foreign tourists could be met and contacts maintained.

So many of those who had benefited from Western education and influence came from the privileged families of nobles or of the very wealthy that Ali Soilih had nowhere to turn to find support for his radical regime except to the students of the *lycée* and to a few radical intellectuals. As has been seen, they proved to be an inadequate basis on which to try to restructure the whole society and economy.

NOTES

1. Sir William Jones, "Remarks on the Island of Hinzuan, or Johanna," *Asiatic Researches* (London, 1807), vol. 2, p. 104.

2. John Fryer, *A New Account of East India and Persia*, W. Crooke, ed., 2 vols. (London: Hakluyt Society, 1909–1915), vol. 1, p. 60.

3. A. Gray, ed., *The Voyage of Francois Pyrard*, 2 vols. (London: Hakluyt Society, 1887–1890), vol. 1, p. 45.

4. H. Chagnoux and A. Haribou, *Les Comores* (Paris: Presses Universitaires de France, 1980), p. 41.

5. A. L. Gevrey, *Essai sur les Comores* (Pondichery: A. Saligny, 1870), p. 140.

6. Chagnoux and Haribou, *Les Comores*, pp. 43–44.

7. The best study of the noble class of the Comoros is Jean Martin, "Les notions des clans, nobles, et notables: leur impact dans la vie politique comorienne d'aujourd'hui," *L'Afrique et l'Asie* 81–82 (1968).

8. Claude Robineau, *Approche sociologique des Comores* (Paris: ORSTOM, 1962), p. 47; Gillian M. Shepherd, "Two Marriage Forms in the Comoro Islands: an Investigation," *Africa* 47 (1977), p. 346.

9. Thierry Flobert, *Les Comores*, Travaux et Mémoires de la Faculté de Droit et de Science Politique d'Aix-Marseille No. 24 (Marseille: Marseille P.U., 1974), pp. 208–218.

10. Ibid., pp. 286–288.

11. Ibid., pp. 195–198.

12. Ibid., pp. 176–182; Du Plantier, *La Grande Comore*, (Paris: Ministère des Colonies, 1904), pp. 32–33. Du Plantier was already lamenting that 15,000 Grande Comorians were living in Zanzibar in 1899.

13. Chagnoux and Haribou, *Les Comores*, p. 87.

14. Sir William Foster, ed., *The Embassy of Sir Thomas Roe* (London: Hakluyt Society, 1899), p. 21.

15. For Islam in the Comoros see Claude Robineau, "L'islam aux Comores: une étude d'histoire culturelle de l'île d'Anjouan," *Arabes et islamisés à Madagascar et dans l'Océan Indien, Revue de Madagascar*, nos. 34, 35, 36, 37 (1966); C. Robineau, *Société et économie d'Anjouan* (Paris: ORSTOM, 1966), pp. 51–71.

16. Anon., "A Visit to the Island of Johanna," *United Service Journal* (1830), no. 1, p. 149.

17. For details of kinship, peer groups, and inheritance see Shepherd, "Two Marriage Forms in the Comoro Islands: an Investigation"; and Robineau, *Société et économie d'Anjouan*, chap. 1, section 2.

18. Shepherd, "Two Marriage Forms in the Comoro Islands: an Investigation," p. 347.

19. For the *mwalimu* see M. Fontoynant and E. Raomandahy, *La Grande Comore*, Mémoires de l'Academie Malgache, fascicule 22 (Tananarive, 1937), pp.

35–39; and Michel Sans, "Les moilimou, sorciers des Comores," *Encyclopédie mensuelle d'outre-mer* 29 (1953), pp. 20–22.

20. Fryer, *A New Account of East India and Persia*, vol. 1, p. 66.

21. Shepherd, "Two Marriage Forms in the Comoro Islands: an Investigation," pp. 352–353.

22. Robineau, *Société et économie d'Anjouan*, p. 80.

23. P. Guy, "Le Mariage en droit comorien," *Revue juridique et politique de l'Union Française* 4 (1958), p. 655.

24. Anon., "A Visit to the Island of Johanna," p. 150.

25. The *grand mariage* played such an important and conspicious part in Comorian life that almost everyone who has written about the islands has had something to say about it. The account that follows is based on the author's own observations made during 1973. See also J. Rouveyran, "Le Dola N'Kou ou grand mariage comorien," *Tiers Monde* 33 (1967); and Shepherd, "Two Marriage Forms in the Comoro Islands: an Investigation."

26. Shepherd, "Two Marriage Forms in the Comoro Islands: an Investigation," p. 350.

27. Anon., "Bâton rompu sur notre culture," *Uhuru* 14 (1973), p. 10, cyclostyled.

28. J-C. Hébert, "Fêtes agraires dans l'île d'Anjouan," *Journal de la société des africanistes* 30 (1960), pp. 101–116.

29. R. C. Temple, ed., *The Travels of Peter Mundy*, 5 vols. (London: Hakluyt Society, 1907–1936), vol. 3, p. 40.

30. Flobert, *Les Comores*, pp. 208–211.

31. "Comoro Islands," *Africa Contemporary Record* 8 (1975–1976), p. B182.

32. Thierry Mantoux, "Notes socio-économiques sur l'archipel des Comores," *Revue française d'études politiques africaines* 100 (1974), p. 43.

5

The Economy of the Comoros

Many island communities throughout the world are in a particular
way the children of the maritime empires. Island groups like the Cape
Verdes, the Azores, the Guinea Islands, the Mascarenes, and the Seychelles
were originally populated by European settlers and their slaves. The
settlers initially came because these islands were important way stations,
and they stayed to develop plantation agriculture on the rich island
soils. The introduction of slaves, the regular visits of ships, and the
residence of garrisons swelled the island populations, which because of
the constant injection of funds from outside, never had to adjust their
way of life to subsistence within the ecological limits of their island
environment. Even when the importance of the islands to the maritime
shipping routes ceased, there was some relief for the populations in
being members of large colonial empires that provided opportunities
for islanders to emigrate and seek employment.

The end of the formal European empires has brought the islands
independence, but as they have been progressively cut off from the
imperial economies that created and once sustained them, their problems
have grown. In many cases shipping services have ceased, subventions
from colonial exchequers have been withdrawn, and in the interests of
genuine independence, foreign military establishments are no longer
welcome. Most serious of all, the opportunities for emigration have been
reduced. The neighboring states, themselves often newly independent,
reserve jobs for their nationals, and world recession in the 1970s and
1980s has limited access to the developed countries of the West. At the
same time the impact of the public-health revolution—the successful
measures taken worldwide to eliminate contagious and infectious diseases—has led to a seemingly uncontrollable mushrooming of population.
Growing population imposes immense strains on the land resources
and on the delicate ecological conditions of island life. It is difficult to
develop industry to the point where it can support a large population
because islands frequently lack natural resources of energy and minerals

95

and their domestic markets are too small to sustain industrial growth. Overpopulation and a deteriorating natural environment, together with the legacy of an economy once geared to the needs of worldwide protectionist empires, make the economic prospects of independent island nations rather bleak.

To a large extent the Comoros fit this pattern, but there is one important distinction; their population is a product of the Muslim rather than the European maritime empires. The length of time that the islands have been settled has meant that a peasant subsistence economy has had time to develop, and for many centuries the relationship between the islands' population and their resources was stable. This stability was seriously upset only with the growth of nineteenth-century capitalism and the colonial take-over. Thereafter, the economic evolution of the Comoros has closely mirrored that of the West Indies, the Cape Verde Islands, and other similar territories.

When the first reliable estimate of the Comorian population was made in 1870, it was thought to number about 65,000. Although there is no way of knowing whether this figure represents a population size of relative stability or whether significant growth had already begun, it is probable that this size of population could maintain itself from domestically grown resources without endangering the ecological balance of the islands. Part of this population was urban and had traditionally engaged in maritime commerce and the servicing of foreign shipping. The rest pursued a form of subsistence agriculture, raising cassava, rice, and bananas, and in the lowland regions, coconuts. To some extent crops were layered. Cassava grew on the ground, and bananas formed an intermediate layer beneath an overhead canopy of forest trees or coconut palms. Growing crops interspersed with trees was well adapted to the ecological needs of the islands. On Grande Comore the almost total lack of any topsoil meant that trees were the only really productive crop, and the preservation of the tree cover on the other islands was essential to stop erosion on the steep mountainsides.[1]

Protein was obtained from cattle, fowl, and fish. The rain forest provided timber needed by the islanders to make furniture and boats. Houses were built either from palm fronds or from lava and coral blocks. The land was owned either by the Arab aristocracy or by village communities. The Arab ruling families farmed their land through a kind of *métayage*, taking a percentage of the crops from the peasants who actually worked the land. The communal land was distributed in small parcels among families who made up the community.

Such a system was able to support a sizable population within the ecological constraints of the four small islands. A relatively stable population was, of course, a prerequisite for the maintenance of such a system, and three factors contributed to population control. First, close control of marriage by village and clan heads meant control of the rate of reproduction. Second, the islands had a high level of infant mortality, and third, many islanders emigrated.

Although the economy of the islanders was largely self-sufficient, there had always been a market sector provided by visiting Arab and European ships to which agricultural surpluses could be sold. Many records indicate that these were exchanged for metal, either worked or in bar form, which constituted the Comorians' principal import. The European India companies undoubtedly enlarged this commerical sector with their demands and probably encouraged the spread of cultivation, but as yet there is no information to establish the extent to which they were responsible for the breakdown of the subsistence economy.

THE ESTABLISHMENT OF THE GREAT LAND COMPANIES

During the nineteenth century, plantation capitalism was introduced on all four of the islands, initially by individual entrepreneurs. Sugar planters from Réunion established a branch of their industry on Mayotte and by the end of the century had eighteen sugar factories in production. On Anjouan William Sunley set up a plantation at Pomoni that became the most profitable in the whole archipelago. Other plantations were established by the sultan himself and at Patsy by an American called Wilson. On Mohéli Joseph Lambert introduced capitalist agriculture, and after his death his concession was taken over by Sunley. On Grande Comore the first planter was Léon Humblot, who pioneered the growing of vanilla.

This phase of capitalism has a number of distinct characteristics. In the early days much depended on the individual ability and drive of the entrepreneur, and the amount of political influence he could wield was crucial to his success. Political influence obtained land (in the case of Lambert and Humblot, as much land as they could use) and also a source of more or less servile labor. The Mayotte planters wielded their political power through the French commandant, who was quite prepared to negotiate labor contracts on their behalf. Sunley, Lambert, and Humblot either obtained laborers directly from the rulers or employed the slaves belonging to Arabs in the islands. The conditions under which contracted laborers were employed and shipped from island to island was little distinguishable from slavery.

The first planters were very wasteful of natural resources. As with the history of sugar cultivation in the West Indies, success in agriculture depended on the natural fertility stored over the centuries in the volcanic soil. The forests were felled, the swamps were drained, and the land was planted until yields began to decline. The major inroads into the rain forest—such a disastrous aspect of the recent history of the islands— were started by the sugar planters.[2] On the other hand, the more enterprising planters began to experiment with new cash crops and to build up the variety of agricultural products that have undoubtedly widened the economic options available to the islanders. Coffee, cacao, vanilla, cloves, sisal, and scent plants were all tried with some success, and some of them established a permanent place for themselves in the Comorian economy.

By the beginning of the twentieth century the planter class was experiencing hard times, and its role was rapidly being supplanted by the better organized and financially more substantial land companies. A few creole families continued to manage plantations. In 1953 H. Isnard described them as follows:

> some fifty *colons* continue to exploit the lands which were conceded to them; half of these are to be found on Grande Comore, the descendants of Léon Humblot among them. Many of them originated in Réunion. There are great disparities in the results they obtain and only a few individual estates bear comparison with those of the companies. Most of the others have reverted to wasteland or have been forfeited, principally in the island of Mohéli where many properties have been left uncultivated and where, according to one report, "Europeans vegetate in sordid misery or have succumbed to an unacceptable promiscuity."[3]

The company that eventually came to dominate the economy of the archipelago originated when the French resident in Anjouan handed over the bankrupt estates of the sultan at Bambao to two Frenchmen, Bouin and Régouin. In 1907 these two entered into a partnership with a M. de Chiris and set up the Société Colonial de Bambao (SCB). The société began a policy of buying up the estates of the *colons* as they came on the market. It successively acquired the concessions of Wilson and Sunley, bought out many of the Mayotte planters, and finally in 1938, took over Humblot's Société de la Grande Comore (SAGC). It has been estimated that at that time the SCB owned 37 percent of the land on Anjouan, 15 percent of Mayotte, 22 percent of Mohéli, and 47 percent of Grande Comore. Even so, the SCB was not the only land company to make good. The Société de Nioumakele became important on Anjouan and the Société des Plants de Parfum de Madagascar was set up on Mayotte, along with a number of others.[4]

These land companies experimented with a wide variety of crops, and by the 1930s a number had successfully established themselves in place of sugar. Vanilla was initially the most profitable, experiencing boom conditions prior to the great depression. Then sisal was grown successfully for a time, and after the war, scent-bearing plants established themselves, with ylang-ylang and jasmine taking pride of place.

Most of these crops were labor intensive, and labor relations became of crucial significance in the history of the companies. In the closing years of the nineteenth century the demands for labor, coupled with the expulsion of Comorians from company land, had been a major cause of social discontent, and disorder had been endemic. In the interests of maintaining reasonable quiet in the islands, the administration had tried to limit some of the pretensions of the companies and concessionaires. Humblot was forced to abandon that condition of his concession that guaranteed his company a supply of labor, and gradually he also had to concede that Comorians could not be expelled from land that they actually occupied. However, he and his heirs fought this issue until 1927, when the SAGC eventually was forced to surrender its claims to some 11,573 hectares (44.68 square miles) that were being farmed by Comorians. In the Comoros the issue of labor was indissolubly linked with that of land, as it was elsewhere in Africa. With so much land at their disposal, the sociétés encouraged a seignorial solution to the problem, allowing peasants to settle on company land provided they and their families worked a certain number of days for the company.[5]

The stranglehold of the companies on the land and people of the islands probably was at its tightest in the years immediately following World War II. In 1939 two companies owned between them 16,873 hectares (65.14 square miles) out of the total area of the island of Anjouan of 42,432 hectares (163.82 square miles). Together with the estates of individual *colons* and the remaining estates of the royal family, some 48 percent of the island was in the hands of large landowners. However, of the island's cultivable land they owned 75 percent. As a result of land reform carried out betwen 1949 and 1953, much land occupied by the villages was transferred into their legal ownership. Even then the land companies continued to own 10,424 hectares (40.25 square miles) on Anjouan and a total of 60,675 hectares (234.26 square miles) in the archipelago as a whole, which amounted to 27 percent of the land area, and white *colons* continued to own a further 5 percent. Isnard recorded in 1953 that on Anjouan some 31,000 people, slightly over half the population, in fact lived in villages on surplus company land. They farmed a mere 2,845 hectares (10.98 square miles) for their support, and only 4,000 of them actually found employment as laborers on the plantations. These workers were given some additional land, which they farmed on a sharecropping basis to help eke out their wages.[6]

Successive land reforms in the 1950s and 1960s gradually transferred some of this land to the peasants, and by 1974, on the eve of the declaration of independence, the 79,000 hectares (305.01 square miles) once owned by the SCB had been reduced to a relatively modest 19,000 hectares (73.35 square miles), although much of this was, of course, the best land. As a measure of control, or some would say complicity, the state had acquired a 26 percent share in the SCB by 1974.

Plantation agriculture made the Comoros a piece in the jigsaw puzzle of international commodity markets. The islands' income came to depend on world markets over which they had no control. Plantation agriculture did not, however, lead to the creation of any of the infrastructure of a modern economy. The companies introduced a certain amount of basic machinery necessary to handle the crops, established their own workshops, and provided their own transport, but apart from these measures they did little. The income derived from selling on the world markets had to pay for the import of almost every article required by the islanders. Two economies therefore grew up side by side: the first, that of the plantation companies and the fringe of French administrators and military personnel who imported all that they required and exported plantation products; the second, the subsistence economy of the native Comorians, increasingly under pressure from loss of land and population growth. The two sectors interlocked only at the level of plantation labor. The system of allowing workers and their families to settle on company land meant that wages were subsidized and kept artificially low because the laborers were able to grow some of their own food. Laboring for the companies did not, therefore, divorce the workers entirely from the life of subsistence farming and did not lead to the emergence of a true rural proletariat.

Few other links between the two economic sectors existed. Retail trade, such as it was, was in the hands of the Indian merchant community whose activities pre-dated the French take-over and who formed part of an older world of Indian mercantile capitalism. A few Comorians, but only a very few, acquired a French education and made some kind of position for themselves within the French empire. Almost without exception these people went abroad and settled in France or Madagascar. The only other link between the sectors was provided by some of the native Comorian landowning aristocracy who began to grow export crops on their land themselves. The early boom in vanilla production between 1910 and 1930 saw, for example, as many as 700 Comorian producers in Grande Comore alone by the year 1921.[7] However, few of these small-scale producers were able to establish themselves, and fewer still had the resources to weather the depression or diversify their production.

POPULATION AND THE SUBSISTENCE ECONOMY

Alienation of land to the plantation companies has not been the only factor to threaten the viability of the subsistence economy of the Comorian peasants. A far greater problem is caused by population growth. Population pressure on the land first became serious in the early years of the twentieth century, but the legal battles fought by Humblot's SAGC against "illegal" squatters on its land made the issue seem to be simply one of land reform. As the companies gradually disgorged some of their unwanted land, it was expected that the population pressure would ease. Few people in the 1930s and 1940s appreciated the nature of the demographic time bomb that was about to explode in the islands.

Gevrey estimated that the population of the islands in 1870 was about 65,000, which would have given a density of 32 people per square kilometer (12.4 per square mile). The next reliable estimate was that made by J. Manicacci in 1935; he put the population at 124,000 or 61.5 people per square kilometer (23.7 per square mile). Already this number

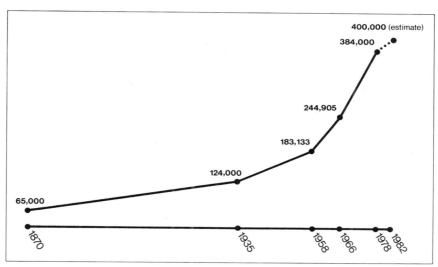

FIGURE 7. Population of the Comoro Islands

was posing a problem, for much of the best land was in the hands of the companies, and large numbers of Comorians were forced to seek work abroad in Madagascar, Zanzibar, and even as far away as the Rand mines in South Africa. When the French took their two official censuses in 1958 and 1966, the population had risen from 183,133 to 244,905[8]—a density of 120 people per square kilometer (46.32 per square mile). At the same time probably as many as 90,000 Comorians were living abroad (approximately 60,000 in Madagascar and 30,000 in East Africa). Although many of the Comorians in East Africa accepted Tanzanian citizenship, a large part of the Madagascan community was repatriated following the troubles in Majunga in 1976. As a result, a further dramatic increase was registered in the census taken in 1978–1979, which put the population of the islands at 384,000 or 189 per square kilometer (72.9 per square mile). See Figure 7.

This population increase has made the Comoros one of the most densely populated parts of the world—with a density that is even greater than it seems because of the large proportion of the landsurface that is uncultivable. In an article published in 1974, Thierry Mantoux estimated that only 48 percent of the land in the islands could be cultivated.[9] If one estimates the population of the islands in 1982 to be approximately 400,000, then the density of people per square kilometer of useable land works out at 505 for Anjouan (194.9 per square mile) and 489 for Grande Comore (188.8 per square mile); the figure for the islands as a whole is 370 (142.8 per square mile). In contrast to these very high densities, Mohéli has only 96 per square kilometer (37.1 per square mile) and Mayotte 215 (82.9 per square mile). Clearly, the pressure

TABLE 1.   Population density of the Comoro Islands
(Based on an estimate of the population in 1982)

	Grande Comore	Anjouan	Mayotte	Moheli	Total
Population	195,500	136,400	51,800	16,300	400,000
Area in km^2	1,148	424	374	290	2,236
Population per km^2	170	322	138	56	179
Percentage of population	49%	34%	13%	4%	100%
Percentage of area	51%	19%	17%	13%	100%
Cultivable area in km^2 (percentage of total)	400 (37%)	270 (25%)	240 (22%)	170 (16%)	1,080 (100%)
Population per km^2 of cultivable land	489	505	215	96	370

The figures are based on calculations contained in Thierry Mantoux, "Notes socio-economiques sur l'archipel des Comores," Revue francaise d'etudes politiques africaines (1974), p. 42, and have been updated to a 1982 estimate for the total population of the islands of 400,000.

points and the real problems are to be found on Anjouan and Grande Comore (see Table 1).

This population growth and high density presents an impossible dilemma. Even if private estates were further broken up and the land distributed among villages, traditional methods of agriculture could not feed such numbers. Food has had to be imported since at least 1960.[10] It is true that much productive land has been given over to growing export crops, and there is one school of thought that says this land should be used for food production. However, if it were, the islands would be left with few means of earning foreign exchange.

There has been some redistribution of population between the islands, and before the Soilih coup peasants from Anjouan and Grande Comore were settling on Mayotte. However, these "emigrants" were expelled after 1976, and only in 1981 did the Mayotte authorities allow some migrant labor to enter from the other islands. At the same time the traditional emigration opportunities to Madagascar and Africa dwindled as those countries pursued policies of employing their nationals. Meanwhile, the population explosion has by no means reached its peak. In 1966 an estimated 44.7 percent of the population was under fifteen years old, and as this group reaches childbearing age, the pace of increase is bound to grow. The Comoros still have a very high rate of infant mortality and low average age of death—a point illustrated by figures published in 1963 that showed only 7.6 percent of the population was over 60 years of age. Once mortality at both ends of the age range begins to decline, the population explosion can be expected to gather still greater momentum.[11]

LAND AND PEASANT FARMING

With the constantly growing pressure of population, land reform has always been considered a high priority. Although major land-reform measures were undertaken in 1928–1930, 1949–1953, and 1972–1973, they did not lead to any very significant redistribution of wealth and provided only the shortest of short-term solutions to the land hunger. After 1912 the French recognized four categories of land: (1) the land of the concession companies—then amounting to 35 percent of the total land surface of the archipelago; (2) state land that comprised much of the forest and the mountainous areas; (3) the private estates of the Comorian aristocracy; and (4) the reserves that the villages owned collectively.

The private landowners and the state allowed Comorian peasants to occupy and farm parts of their land, sometimes in return for rent, at other times in exchange for their labor. The so-called land reforms that took place were legal recognition of the land titles of peasants who were already in occupation and were farming the land. The reforms did not, by and large, make more land available for peasant occupation. Land reforms were introduced to damp down the danger of rural unrest, and one historian has described them as important principally from the psychological and juridical rather than economic point of view. By the time of independence little had been achieved toward redressing the inequalities that existed between the large landowners, many of them absentees, and the small-scale subsistence farmers.

Moreover, with every redistribution of land the agrarian patchwork of the islands became more complex. New land was made available to villages on a collective basis. The villages divided the land among those in need, who in turn were able to treat it as a private holding. Then, when the 1949–1953 land reform took place, although much of the land went to squatters who were already in possession, inevitably some peasants were evicted as the land passed to different villages. Nor was the village land necessarily immediately adjacent to the village, and the fields of the villagers might lie an hour's walk away or more, forcing the unfortunate peasant farmer to trudge through the fertile fields of private landowners to his sterile mountain plot.

The land problem has not simply been one of crude land shortage; it has also been a matter of land quality and of agricultural technique. The staple crops of the Comorians are maize, cassava, mountain rice, and coconuts, with onions, bananas, tomatoes, peas, etc. grown to supplement them. The coconut grows only in the lowland zone below the 1,000-foot contour and provides food and building materials and is a cash crop. However, much of the peasant land is situated on the misty mountain slopes too high for coconut cultivation. Here the staple crop is mountain rice, which farmers have to grow, as often as not, on very steep slopes. The typical cycle of mountain agriculture for a Comorian farmer used to be to move into an area of forest, clear the undergrowth, and plant bananas. Beneath these, cassava roots could be cultivated. A year or two later the remaining trees would be felled and the slopes planted with rice. After a season or two the ground had to be abandoned because of exhaustion. As this prolonged cycle is no longer possible in most areas, the burning of surface vegetation remains the commonest way of preparing fields; tractors and draught animals are practically unknown, and there is little use of manure. Crop yields continually fall as the periods of fallow become shorter and shorter. Rice, the food crop on which the majority of Comorians depend, has suffered particularly badly, and yields are less than a quarter of those obtained in nearby Madagascar. Moreover, on the heavily cropped hillsides, water erosion can be devastating. Erosion has already reached extreme proportions in many parts of the archipelago, and its effects can be seen most vividly in the villages themselves. The paths between the houses become torrents during the rains, and ravines are rapidly scoured out, leaving the huts precariously perched on cliffs of bare earth.

The islanders undoubtedly have a problem obtaining sufficient protein. There are thought to be about 75,000 head of cattle and 40,000 goats in the islands, but although Mohéli and Mayotte are adequately stocked, Anjouan in particular is very short, having only 16 percent of the cattle and 7.6 percent of the goats.[12] Increasing the amount of the livestock presents obvious difficulties. Grande Comore has relatively little land suitable for pasture, and the other islands can only increase pasture at the expense of other crops.

The subsistence economy of the Comoros is now near total collapse. For the last twenty years the islanders have been consistently unable to supply their basic foodstuffs. Food imports constitute up to 40 percent of the total import bill, and dependence on imported rice, which is the staple food, has grown to the point that five times as much rice is imported as is grown in the islands.[13] As far as statistics go (and they are particularly unreliable for the period after independence in 1975), figures show food production stagnating at best and in decline when measured as output per capita.

FISHING

Fishing would seem to be the obvious way for an island people to supplement its diet and earn a cash income. The catching of fish is an ancient craft in the Comoros and still preserves its traditional ways. It is practiced by only a small section of the population, which forms a distinct class occupying its own villages or its own quarter in the towns. Most fishermen are also farmers, and they fish simply to supplement their own diet. A recent estimate suggests that there may be perhaps 3,500 fishermen,[14] mostly part-time, but this number represents a tiny proportion of the population, even of those who live immediately by the sea.

N'tsaoueni (Grande Comore): The fishing fleet

Fish are still caught in a wholly traditional manner—by trailing a baited line from an outrigger canoe. Nets are seldom used because of the problems caused by coral outcrops. The canoes, although remarkably seaworthy, cannot venture out in rough weather, and fishermen can be confined to shore for many days. Some go out at night, attracting fish by hanging a small gasoline lamp from a pole in the canoe. It is not uncommon to see a whole line of these lights offshore on a calm night. Although some canoes can be fitted with sails, it is still very unusual for any of them to have an outboard motor.

The canoes are made from a single tree trunk and are fitted with one or two outriggers. The double outrigger is used exclusively on Grande Comore and where Grande Comorian fishermen have settled on the other islands. The single outrigger predominates on Anjouan and Mohéli and is the only sort to be used on Mayotte. Canoes represent a large investment for fishermen—in 1972 a canoe could cost the equivalent of £50–70, and they are usually short-lived. After a life of three to five years the hull tends to split. The rapid exhaustion of the forests on the islands endangers the ancient craft of canoe construction, for the large, full-grown forest trees used for the canoes will soon no longer be found.[15]

The potential for developing a fishing industry in the Comoros and for putting the importers of Moroccan sardines out of business is not as great as it might seem. The Mayotte reef is rich in fish, but otherwise the waters around the islands are deep, and there are few

N'tsaoueni (Grande Comore): The double outrigger canoe

banks or valuable fishing grounds. Even so, it has been estimated that within a radius of 50 kilometers (31.25 miles) the sea of the archipelago could yield 20,000 tonnes (19,684 tons) of fish a year, compared to the 5,000 tonnes (4,921 tons) taken today. All this, however, depends on investment in ocean-going fishing vessels and on fish storage and canning facilities, both of which have been planned but have not yet materialized.[16]

AGRICULTURAL EXPORTS

If food now regularly forms 40 percent or more of all imports, cash crops make up 90 percent of all exports. Sugar was the first significant export from the islands, but it declined in importance and eventually disappeared, and today sugar is imported by the Comoros. Sugar was succeeded by coffee, cacao, vanilla, scent essences, and sisal.[17] In 1953 the Comoros were producing 2,000 tonnes (1968.4 tons) of sisal a year, but this industry also has gone into decline due to world surpluses and the deleterious effect that the crop has on the soil. Today the islands produce no sisal at all. Since 1960 concentration has been on the production of cloves, vanilla, copra, and scent essences. Table 2 shows the percentage of total exports made up by each of these four commodities. The figures for the years 1977–1980 are estimates, as no reliable statistics were kept during those years. The Soilih government did not keep statistics, and the restored regime of Ahmed Abdullah issued no reliable figures between 1978 and 1981. The figures given in Table 2 illustrate

Table 2. Cash crops as percentages of total exports

	1970	1971	1972	1973	1974	1975	1976	1977	1978	1979	1980
Vanilla	31.5	38.5	40.6	9.0	22.1	33.8	20.9	49.2	35.0	60.6	8.4
Ylang-ylang	26.2	22.4	33.1	51.5	36.7	25.2	27.8	26.6	30.3	18.9	21.3
Copra	15.5	13.1	6.0	20.7	23.2	4.5	5.5	6.6	9.7	6.9	6.0
Cloves	17.4	17.1	10.9	7.9	11.3	28.8	36.5	13.3	21.5	11.9	60.2
Totals	90.6	91.1	90.6	89.1	93.3	92.3	90.7	95.1	96.5	98.3	95.9

Note: figures from 1977-1980 exclude Mayotte and are estimates only.

Sources: Claude Gaspart, "The Comoro Islands Since Independence: An Economic Appraisal," Proceedings of the ICIOS Conference, Perth, 1979, p. 10. The Comoros: Current Economic Situation and Prospects (Washington, D.C.: World Bank, 1983), p. 150.

well the way these four commodities dominate the export sector, the decline in the importance of copra being, perhaps, the only trend of major significance. Yet during this period there was an important change in the way many of these crops were produced as the large companies increasingly left primary production to small-scale enterprise and concentrated on processing and marketing. The increasing role of peasants and small farmers in production is clearly of major importance for the future of the Comoros and needs to be examined in more detail.

A variety of scent-producing plants has been tried with greater or lesser success.[18] Cassia and palmarosa were introduced in the 1920s and 1930s, and more recently there have been experiments with jasmine. Other scent plants still in the experimental stage or already cultivated are basilic, patchouli, cinnamon flower, tuberose, and flowers of clove. Lemongrass was also grown at one time. The most important of the scent plants, however, is ylang-ylang. This plant was introduced into the islands by the French early in the twentieth century, and by the middle of the 1970s the Comoros were producing 70 percent of the world's supply of ylang-ylang oil. All of it was being sold to the French scent industry. The trees are trained like vines after they have grown to be about five feet tall. Their tortured branches and twisted stems are one of the commonest sights in the islands. The flowers are a greenish color, and their scent is extremely powerful, filling the whole air of the islands after a rainstorm. Picking ylang-ylang flowers is labor intensive, and the job is usually performed by female workers.

There are three main techniques for extracting the scent essences: extraction by steam, extraction by using alcohol or some other spirit, and extraction by heating the flowers in oil. The preliminary processing has to be carried out in the islands shortly after the flowers have been picked, but no scents are actually manufactured in the Comoros.

Copra and cloves were also originally introduced as plantation crops on the large estates of the concession companies. Once again the preliminary processing, in this case drying, has to take place soon after harvest, but no further manufacturing is carried out in the islands.

Until recently it was received wisdom that export crops of high quality could only be grown on large plantations that were backed with adequate capital and had the resources to tide the industry over bad years. It was argued that only large plantations were capable of creating the infrastructure required by a developing economy and that large producers could control marketing and production in order to prevent a glut in the market and a collapse in prices. These arguments would not still be seriously advanced if they did not contain some truth. However, it has become clear in recent years that all cash crops of the Comoros can be grown as satisfactorily by peasants as by concession companies. Clove trees can be seen growing singly in the villages, and in August it is common to see their brightly colored keys spread out to blacken in the sun. Small-scale copra production also takes place in the villages, and ylang-ylang trees will grow as well on their own as in plantations. Small steam distilleries operate in some of the towns—built of old oil drums and bent copper pipes and looking like Heath Robinson originals. However, it was in vanilla production that the hold of the companies was first broken, because theft of vanilla was so easy. By the 1970s most companies had ceased producing vanilla and concentrated instead on the control of marketing.

What began with vanilla spread to other commodities. The companies shifted the emphasis of their activities from production to collection and marketing. Increasingly ylang-ylang trees and coconut palms were leased out to peasants, and the companies bought the produce, or itinerant *collecteurs* and Indian storekeepers purchased the product of small-scale peasant production for sale to the companies.[19] The logical extension of this process is for state-run growers' cooperatives eventually to take over collection and marketing, though overseas sales will still, no doubt, lie beyond Comorian control. Such a move was attempted during the government of Ali Soilih, but the return to power of Ahmed Abdullah is the return of a man who made his fortune in vanilla trading; one of the first acts of his government was to introduce regulations that effectively confined the sale of vanilla to a handful of privileged exporters.

It was the realization that the role of the concession company in primary production was declining, coupled with unmistakable signs of rural unrest, that led to the land reforms of 1972–1973 that again transferred much surplus company land to the villages and to private buyers.

However, debate is not confined to the issue of whether export crops should be grown by plantation companies or by peasants. The issue now is whether land should be devoted to these crops at all. During the decade prior to 1975 when the French initiated some research and development programs through agencies like FIDES (Fonds de Developpement Economique et Social) and SODEC (Société pour le Developpement Economique des Comores), the assumption clearly was made that the economic future of the islands would lie with their export crops. With the population of the islands rapidly rising, however, and with food imports now dominating the balance of payments, it has been strongly urged, initially by the left but now by politicans of all persuasions, that the first priority for the islands is to become self-sufficient in food production, rather than that they should earn foreign exchange by the production of commodities for which there are rapidly being developed alternative sources of supply and synthetic substitutes. In pursuit of greater self-sufficiency, the European Development Fund began in 1978 to finance a maize project. The object of this was to grow maize and peas on most of the 9,300 hectares (22,971 acres) at present given over to rice cultivation. The heavier yield of these crops was expected to increase cereal production in the islands by 28,000 tonnes (27,558 tons). Popular taste in food was to be influenced by raising taxes on rice consumption. However, if the goal of self-sufficiency in food were to be vigorously pursued, the problem of earning foreign exchange would remain and could only be met by developing tourism or the industrial sector; and it is just in these areas that the economy of the islands is weakest.

INDUSTRY

Industry, like agriculture, can be divided into traditional and modern sectors. Traditional crafts in the Comoros are simple and are directly connected with the needs of the community. There are carpenters and builders, experts in the burning of coral to make lime, and experts in the making of the wooden doors and windows that still grace the townhouses of the wealthy. In the villages the houses are constructed either of plaited coconut fronds that are set on simple square frames and thatched, or in the higher regions where coconut palms do not grow, of wood and grass thatch. Baskets and panniers of all shapes, sizes, and for all uses are woven, and ropes are twisted from coir. The coconut palm also provides the wherewithal to make hats, mats, and sandals. Very little pottery is produced, and one has to travel to Fumboni in the south of Grande Comore or to Wani on Anjouan to find traditional, indigenous pottery making still being practiced.

The art of the goldsmith is highly esteemed and is practiced both in modern workshops equipped with up-to-date machinery and in the poorest surroundings, where the craftsman can sometimes be seen seated at the door of a hut, working the gold with a stone hammer. At one time weaving and primitive sugar boiling were practiced, and boats were built and repaired on the beaches where aged craftsmen can be seen tinkering with lighters and small dhows. Canoes, of course, are still constructed in considerable numbers. In 1974 Thierry Mantoux gave exact figures for the numbers of artisans, derived presumably from the most recent census, but with what real accuracy it is impossible to say. There were 1,080 woodworkers, 1,600 tailors, 340 needlewomen (*brodeuses*), 470 rope-makers, 60 net-makers, 15 doll-makers, 70 metalworkers (*forgeurs*), 30 jewellers, 30 potters, 15 shoemakers and 1,800 basket-makers.[20]

On this traditional industrial base virtually nothing has been built. A hundred years ago Gevrey complained that the planters of Mayotte imported everything they needed for their plantations, and today the islands still import everything except the simplest products of the traditional economy. Until 1949 all that had been done to create the infrastructure of a modern economy had been the provision of the bare essentials for the islands' security: landing strips, piers, and a few government buildings. Each plantation installed whatever power and transport it required. Then in 1949, the first four-year plan, designed to improve the basic infrastructure, was launched. This plan was followed by two more four-year plans aimed at rural development. The results were not impressive, and it was only in the late 1960s, under the impetus of the Common Market Regional Fund, that real progress was made. Even so, the backwardness of the islands was such that comparatively little infrastructure had been developed at the time of the islands' independence in 1975. Independence opened up many fresh sources of aid, but these rapidly withdrew during the Soilih regime, with the result that by the end of the 1970s the islands were still not equipped with many of the most elementary necessities for a modern economy.

In particular the Comoros have suffered from poor transport. The grading and tarring of roads only began in the late 1960s, and by the time of independence few parts of the archipelago were readily accessible to motor vehicles. On Grande Comore a tarred motor road ran from Mitsamiouli down the whole western side of the island to Fumboni, but the eastern side, including the large town of M'Beni, was without any access except by a rocky track passable only to trucks and landrovers. On Anjouan roads had been engineered from Mutsammudu across passes of almost alpine proportions to Domoni and Sima, but the whole southwest coast and the northern and southern peninsulas, among the most populous parts of the island, were still cut off. On Mayotte and Mohéli the problem was even worse. Each had a single tarred road crossing the center of the island, but in the case of Mohéli the road did not run near any centers of population and petered out in the bush without arriving at any destination. In 1978 official figures credited the islands with a total of 402 kilometers (251 miles) of tarred road (210 kilometers [131 miles] on Grande Comore) and a further 138 kilometers (86 miles) under construction.[21] Tarred roads are of particular significance for the Comoros because on the steep, mountainous terrain the heavy tropical rain easily washes away dirt roads and renders them impassable.

Historically the Comoro islanders have been traders and seafarers as well as peasant farmers. Fishing apart, however, the sea now appears to play little part in the economy of the islands. During the last years of direct French rule no boats called at the islands at all with the exception of one or two rusty cargo ships that stopped on their runs between Dar es Salaam and Majunga. The Messageries Maritimes liners ceased service early in the 1960s, and the French substituted for them a regular air link. Flights from Tananarive and Paris reached the island once or twice a week, but the long-distance jets could only land at Moroni or on Pamanzi Island off Mayotte, which also served as a military aerodrome. Even these airfields could not handle the larger jets, and work began on an international airfield at Hahaia twenty miles from Moroni that was completed in 1975, although it did not immediately come into use due to lack of equipment. Meanwhile, shipping between the islands ceased altogether and contact was only maintained by daily flights made by two antique DC4s operated by a French company calling itself Air Comore. These aircraft carried passengers and some random cargo. It was not uncommon for two or three blocks of seats to be removed and for a car or light van to be hoisted on board by the strong arms of the airport staff. Although this daily flight provided the only regular contact between the islands, a round-trip ticket to all four islands in 1973 cost the equivalent of £32—twice the annual income of the average Comorian.

The improvement of shipping services presents some real problems. At the time of independence ships of more than four meters (13.12 feet) draught could not enter the harbor at Moroni, and neither Mutsammudu nor Fomboni (the capital of Mohéli) had any harbor at all.[22] Instead, each had a jetty built from the beach into the sea at which small boats could tie up, but which otherwise served as a landing place for lighters unloading from ships anchored offshore. Only Mayotte had a deepwater harbor that could take ships of any size and that was sheltered from the monsoon. There were no port facilities in the bay of Pamanzi, and after the declaration of independence in 1975 the island remained under direct French administration and was of no use to the rest of the archipelago. Urgent studies concerning the extension of Mutsammudu were begun in 1973, but this work, like so much else, was interrupted by the Soilih coup. In 1983, when the World Bank Report was published, there was little progress to announce beyond the existence of paper plans to improve three of the ports of the archipelago and buy an inter-island ferry.

The relative isolation of one island from another within the archipelago has obviously hindered the growth of a domestic market and at the same time has deepened the political separatist tendencies natural among island communities.

What at first sight is difficult to explain is the lack of traditional small craft plying between the islands. The fact is, however, that few of these boats now exist in seaworthy condition. The lack of capital undoubtedly lies at the root of the difficulty; and for those Comorians with capital there are more lucrative outlets than small-scale shipping. Clearly the government should have established a ferry service years ago, but such a service would have undermined the monopoly of Air Comore, which has always had enough influence to scotch any suggestion of the opening of a sea route.

At the time of independence other aspects of the economic infrastructure remained even more rudimentary. The islands were connected by telephone with Paris and Tananarive, but telex was only introduced in 1977.[23] Apart from lines connecting the main towns there were no internal telephone services. Electricity was installed in the island capitals, and some French establishments had their own generators, but all the rural areas were without power. There was no running water outside the main towns, and the capital, Moroni, was only given a permanent water supply with the drilling of a successful borehole at Vouvouni in

1976. Banking and postal services existed to any regular extent only in Moroni, the other towns having to make do with agencies that transacted very little business. This lack of infrastructure is both cause and effect of a corresponding lack of a modern sector in the economy.

In 1974 the number of wage earners in the islands reached a peak of about 15,000. Two years earlier there had been 13,310, which represented 4.6 percent of the population as a whole and 9.8 percent of the economically active population. The vast majority (78.3 percent) of these lived on the islands of Grande Comore and Anjouan, which were the most developed economically and the most populous, but it was on Mohéli alone that wage earners formed a substantial proportion (16.4 percent) of the economically active population. Of the total number of wage earners, only 19.6 percent were involved in industry or construction and a mere 3 percent (403 people) in manufacturing industry or workshops. These figures speak for themselves. At the time of independence there was simply no industrial sector at all. The islands had to import virtually every manufactured article, including such things as soap, salt, sugar, softdrinks, and canned fish, all of which could easily have been made from locally produced ingredients. Since independence little has changed. A softdrinks factory and a soap factory have been started, and there has been some reinvestment in the plant needed for the processing of exports like ylang-ylang and vanilla. A print works and some modern sawmills have been built—but that is all, despite the formal establishment of the Development Bank.

This complete lack of any modern sector of the economy might be attributed simply to the extreme distortions forced on the islands by the colonial plantation economy. A similar pattern can be seen, for example, in the areas where large plantations were established in the Portuguese colonies. However, it is important not to seek too simplistic an explanation, for there are other causes of this backwardness. The decay of inter-island shipping, for example, occurred in the middle years of the nineteenth century and was clearly related to the decline in the slave trade. Likewise, the lack of capital investment and capital accumulation is, at least in part, the result of the conspicuous expenditure associated with traditional Muslim marriages. Equally serious is the problem of establishing a domestic market among island communities separated from one another either by the sea or by steep mountains, and where retailing is in the hands of an Indian elite whose commercial dominance was accepted by the colonial regime.

As the industrial sector is tiny, it is to be expected that the other modern sectors of the economy will also be small in scale. In the private sector 15.8 percent of wage earners are employed in construction, much of which is done by wholly traditional methods. A further 10.3 percent work in retailing, banking, and commerce. Transport, significantly, employs only 5.4 percent and tourism a mere 1.1 percent.[24]

EXTERNAL TRADE AND FINANCE

With a rapidly growing population that can no longer feed itself by traditional methods, with a plantation economy that is at best static, and with virtually no industrial sector, the financial position of the Comoro Islands can be easily imagined. Until the 1960s it was French policy to keep the trade of the islands more or less in balance and the budget breaking even. This was achieved by reducing to a minimum investment and the import of machinery, construction materials, etc., and by encouraging large-scale emigration both to relieve the pressure of population in the islands and to secure a flow of foreign earnings in the form of remittances.[25]

After 1960 this picture began to change. Foreign investment in the Comoros, and hence imports, began to rise. Madagascar, newly independent in 1960, began to limit immigration and also sent Comorians back to the islands, a process that speeded up after the fall of President Tsiranana in 1972 and culminated in mass expulsions in 1977. At the same time the Comoro government, having made itself independent of France politically, tried to make itself independent financially as well. The Comoros, therefore, began to pursue development policies at a time when remittances from emigrants were drying up and when the balance of trade was becoming increasingly adverse to the islands. At the same time, for political reasons, financial aid from France was temporarily cut off.

Trade deficits began to open alarmingly. In 1960 exports covered 84 percent of imports; in 1970 they covered 54 percent, and in 1975 they covered only 41 percent. The worst year was 1973 when exports covered only 33 percent of imports (see Table 3).[26] The trade deficit was clearly the result of the increase in imports, particularly food imports. Throughout the 1970s between 30 and 40 percent of all imports was food, and in 1974 exports failed even to cover the cost of food imports alone.

An analysis of imports unmistakably shows how development is made impossible by the growing food deficit. In 1970 only 10 percent of imports consisted of industrial or agricultural machinery, while over 36 percent consisted of food. In 1975 still only 12.3 percent of imports consisted of machinery and 28.9 percent of food.[27] A list of imports for 1975, the last year for which complete and accurate statistics exist, is given in Table 4, with World Bank estimates for 1979 by way of comparison. Trade deficits of this kind can be made up in one of three ways: remittances, tourism, or foreign aid. Up until 1975 the Comoros had to rely largely on French aid to cover the deficit. Trade was overwhelmingly with the franc-zone countries of France and Madagascar, and in 1970 no less than 87.7 percent of imports came from the franc zone, and 57.8 percent of exports went there.[28] French aid also covered the budgetary deficits, and in 1975 it was estimated that French aid

Table 3. Value of exports and imports with indices, 1970-1980. (In millions of CFA; figures in parentheses express values as percentages of 1970 statistics. Figures for 1977-1980 are estimates only and do not include Mayotte)

	1970	1971	1972	1973	1974	1975	1976	1977	1978	1979	1980
Imports	2,373 (100%)	2,835 (119%)	2,849 (120%)	3,369 (142%)	6,203 (266%)	4,975 (210%)	3,119 (131%)	4,053 (171%)	4,330 (182%)	6,506 (274%)	9,015 (380%)
Exports	1,278 (100%)	1,572 (123%)	1,511 (118%)	1,106 (87%)	2,138 (167%)	2,036 (159%)	2,224 (174%)	2,203 (172%)	2,103 (165%)	3,745 (293%)	2,282 (179%)

Source: Claude Gaspart, "The Comoro Islands since Independence: An Economic Appraisal," Proceedings of the ICIOS Conference, Perth, 1979, p. 13. The Comoro Islands: Current Economic Situation and Prospects (Washington, D.C.: World Bank, 1983), pp. 150, 152.

Table 4.   Imports in millions of CFA in 1975 and 1979

	1975	1979*
Meat	130.8	547.4
Rice	738.4	1091.7
Flour	92.2	125.4
Sugar	84.1	264.6
Misc. (salt, oil, etc.)	393.9	249.0
Cigarettes	47.0	79.5
Pharmaceuticals	147.9	125.1
Textiles	283.2	534.7
Cars	97.7	398.4
Misc. finished products	1013.1	838.4
Petroleum	448.7	385.4
Farm Equipment	38.6	--
Industrial equipment	573.0	--
Capital goods	--	665.3
Cement	251.3	145.4
Galvanized iron sheets	101.7	--
Iron bars	83.0	--
Raw materials, etc.	450.0	--
Iron and Steel	--	520.7
Products of organic origin	--	5.0
Mineral products	--	3.0
Misc.	--	500.0
Total	4,974.6	6,506.0

*Figures for 1979 refer to three islands and are estimates only.

Sources: Claude Gaspart, "The Comoro Islands since Independence: An Economic Appraisal," in Section II of the ICIOS Conference, Perth, 1979, p. 12.   The Comoro Islands: Current Economic Situation and Prospects (Washington, D.C.: World Bank, 1983), p. 152.

provided three-quarters of the total Comorian budget, both current expenditure and investment.

It is difficult to imagine a dependence more complete than that represented by these figures, yet the situation of the Comoros is by no means unique. The Seychelle Islands have a similar type of economy and share in many of the basic problems of the Comoros. Moreover, their trade deficit is very much larger; in 1980 only 5.2 percent of imports were covered by export earnings. However, the Seychelles can afford a trade deficit of this magnitude because of their earnings from tourism.[29] Tourism is also an important earner of foreign exchange for Mauritius, Kenya, and other Indian Ocean countries. On the face of it, there is no reason why the Comoros should not also enjoy considerable foreign-exchange earnings from tourism.

Foreign tourists, however, play almost no part in the economy of the islands. Late in the 1960s the government and private investors began to put a certain effort into developing tourism. Government-financed hotels were built at Mutsammudu and at Moroni, and private beach developments grew up at Mitsamiouli and on Mohéli's picturesque western coast. Some restaurants also made an appearance, and a few parties of Americans stopped briefly on their way around the world. By the early 1970s there were probably 3,000 tourists a year visiting the islands, and there were 209 hotel beds available in the archipelago. From then on tourism flagged, and the period of the revolutionary government of Ali Soilih put an end to it altogether. After Abdullah's restoration a state company took over four of the hotels, but of 1,300 visitors recorded in 1979, 90 percent were businessmen.[30] The failure of tourism to develop as an industry has a number of causes. Although the islands have many tropical charms, there are relatively few good beaches in the Comoros, except on the inaccessible coasts of Mohéli. Grande Comore in particular has a rocky, lava coast with little sand, the same rock formation that leaves the island with very little fresh water. The attractions of the islands for tourists are chiefly scenic or else they lie in such special features as the Karthala Volcano or the Mayotte barrier reef, both of which are inaccessible to all but the dedicated few. The lack of good roads or any form of transport except taxis makes it extremely difficult for tourists to travel around.

However, there appears to be another reason for the failure of tourism: Neither the French nor the Comorian politicians have ever really believed in the ability of tourism to solve the islands' economic problems. Tourism brings foreign exchange, but much that tourists spend their money on has to be imported, and employment is created only for waiters, barmen, taxidrivers, and purveyors of a few other services. Moreover, the industry would have to invest heavily before it could even hope to rival the well-established tourist attractions of neighboring Indian Ocean countries. Whatever the reasons, and Muslim cultural conservatism may be among them, Comorians of both the left and the right have largely discounted tourism and ignored its potential.

POST INDEPENDENCE

The Comoros declared their independence from France in July 1975 at a time when three-quarters of all government expenditure derived from French aid. The immediate consequence was the division of the

archipelago, since France retained control of Mayotte, and the interruption
of aid and development programs. A month later, in August, a further
coup placed Ali Soilih and his mentor, Said Ibrahim, at the head of the
government. Within a year Said Ibrahim was dead, and Ali Soilih,
having severed all economic ties with France, had embarked on an
ambitious economic and social revolution. The revolutionary government
was guided by the ideas that the socialists of PASOCO had used to
analyze the economic problems of the Comoros. The PASOCO socialists
had identified as the principal problems the inability to grow enough
food and the stultifying effects of Islamic conservatism. Food imports
were absorbing all the foreign-exchange earnings, while conservative
social customs led to all available capital being directed toward the
lavish expenditure of the *grand mariage*. Whatever else it may have
achieved, the *grand mariage* beggared the population and diverted capital
from economic investment. A further problem was the size of the central
administration, which in 1970 absorbed 54 percent of the budget.[31]

The revolutionary reforms of Soilih's government sought to de-
centralize government and to base education, administration, and economic effort on local units, moudiryias, of not more than eight to nine
thousand people. Food self-sufficiency was to be a priority and was to
be achieved in part by devoting foreign exchange to the import of
agricultural machinery, and in part by dividing the remaining estates
of the land companies into half-acre lots for the landless. The feudal
domains of Comorian landowners were also divided up. At the same
time state corporations were established to handle imports and exports.
Social reform concentrated on outlawing the *grand mariage* and the
whole paraphernalia of Islamic marriage, including the wearing of the
veil, which symbolized the economic immobilization of middle-class
women.[32]

As Soilih's revolution proceeded on its intoxicating way, a hurricane
of events swamped the frail craft of the Comorian state. In December
1976 rioting in Majunga, Madagascar, led to a massacre of Comorians
and the decision by Soilih to repatriate a large part of the Comorian
community. In all, something like 17,000 refugees returned to the islands.
In the same year, 1977, the economic life of Grande Comore was
dislocated by a major eruption of Karthala, which poured its lava into
the sea down the populous side of the island. Aid for food and emergency
housing was urgently sought from the international community, and
some supplies did arrive, but by this time Soilih had disbanded the
central administration and there was no machinery left to organize the
distribution of aid. The islands began to live in a haphazard, hand-to-
mouth fashion. Exports slumped disastrously—but no statistics of any
kind were compiled, and the extent of the economic chaos can only be
imagined. Mohéli and Anjouan experienced an outbreak of separatist
revolts, at least in part reflecting the exasperation of a conservative
peasantry and their determination to resist further disruption.[33]

Soilih's revolution had reached the peak of its "destructive" phase (colonial land companies partially expropriated, civil service disbanded, French economic protection rejected) and its constructive phase existed only on paper when the regime was overthrown by Denard's mercenaries in May 1978. The restored president, Ahmed Abdullah, devoted the next two years to setting the economic and social clock back, restoring the landowners and companies, denationalizing the state corporations, allowing Islamic conservatism full rein, and rebuilding economic bridges with the French.

Aid programs began to mushroom on all sides once it was clear that the unpredictable Soilih was gone and a familiar and stable "protected" neo-colonial regime was in power. As preliminary studies have been completed, funds have arrived earmarked for harbors, airfields, fisheries, roads, and education. Relations with France were quickly reestablished but a characteristic of the post-Soilih era has been the attempt to diversify the sources of economic aid. The Comoros have moved closer to their African neighbors, a trend established in the Soilih years when Tanzania showed itself to be one of the few friends the islands possessed. Feelers have also been put out in the direction of the Arab states of the Gulf, and loans have been received from Kuwait and Saudi Arabia as well as from the Arab Development Fund. Canada, Belgium, and Switzerland have also given aid, again a legacy of the Soilih years when, unexpectedly, these impeccably capitalist countries stepped into the economic gap left by the retreating French. However, the World Bank Report, which was published in 1983, drew attention to the problems connected with the proper utilization of aid. Although Soilih was gone and the civil service had been reincarnated, there was a lack of technical and administrative expertise at all levels; not enough accountants to keep the books of state enterprises or tax officials to make more than the crudest effort to collect taxes; government departments and state-owned companies unable to pay each others' bills; not even enough secretearies to staff the various offices; and to cap it all, a federal structure of government with two administrative layers duplicating each other's work. These are some of the realities of the situation that would-be donors have to face.[34]

THE ECONOMIC PROSPECTS OF THE ISLANDS

It is easy to pillory the Soilih years for their chaos and political violence and for the discontinuities that undoubtedly brought much poverty and suffering. As the *Africa Contemporary Record* put it:

> The penurious indigenous economy thus remains substantially unchanged from what it had always been. The difference is that penury has now become the *national* economy, that more Comorians are condemned to live with it than ever before, and that there is no contiguous colonial economy to provide a basis for comparison.[35]

Nevertheless, it is difficult not to conclude that much of the Soilih program was highly relevant to the needs of the islands. Self-sufficiency in food, for example, must be a high priority, but there are formidable ecological reasons why this goal cannot be achieved simply through the expansion of traditional agriculture. Traditional farming methods were successful when there was abundance of land and when forest cover in the mountains retained moisture and prevented soil erosion. However, the forests have been rapidly felled to provide extra farmland, and since 1950 as much as 50 percent of the forests may have disappeared.[36] The slopes of Karthala probably contain the last remaining major area of rain forest. Erosion and desiccation resulting from this destruction are clearly reaching disastrous proportions in some parts of the islands, and more intensive cultivation would only hasten disaster. The alternative is to make farming more capital intensive through a higher input of fertilizer, but it is the capital that would buy this fertilizer that the islands so signally lack.

The attainment of self-sufficiency in food is rendered an impossibility, while the population expansion continues unabated. The Comoros appear to be in an early stage of the cycle of population growth, having only recently begun to check the major diseases leading to high mortality. In the normal course of events a period of rapid population expansion can now be expected, with an increasing number of children surviving infancy and growing to child-bearing age. Moreover, none of the conditions exist that might lead to slower growth: Living standards are exceptionally low; most of the population is engaged in subsistence agriculture in communities where children are a labor force and a means of insurance; and religious conservatism inhibits any campaign for birth control. In the past population pressures found an outlet in emigration. However, not only is that outlet now stopped, but the return of past emigrants is seriously exacerbating the problem that already exists.

If food self-sufficiency is a receding dream, the islands must earn foreign exchange in order to import food. Traditionally the main exports have been plantation crops, which are increasingly threatened by rival producers and synthetic substitutes. EEC agreements now support the prices of cloves, ylang-ylang, copra, and vanilla, and there is some chance the Comoros may hang on to the export markets it now has. However, investment is needed to maintain the quality and output of these crops and to ensure that as much of the processing work as possible is done in the islands.

Apart from some windfall like the discovery of oil reserves, there are only two other ways in which foreign exchange can be earned—industry and tourism. If communications and retailing were improved, the islands would form a market large enough to support a number of import-saving consumer industries—for example, production of soap, candles, softdrinks, canned fish, sugar, and salt. Other plans, already submitted to the Development Bank, include factories for sandals, jeans, paint, and mattresses. However, land would need to be made over for the production of the constituent raw materials of most of these products. Moreover, it is unlikely that these industries would ever acquire much significance as exports, for the surrounding countries of the western Indian Ocean all have similar agricultural economies and develop similar industries.

Industrial development might, however, be specifically oriented toward export. The prospect for this is slim at present. Raw materials would have to be imported and the markets for the finished products are all distant. Also, although abundant cheap labor is available, the population at present is so clearly lacking in education and industrial skills and the islands themselves are so totally without the most basic economic infrastructure that they are unlikely to rival the attractions of Hong Kong or the Philippines for the foreseeable future.

Tourism remains the most easily realizable asset and earner of foreign exchange, but as already discussed, even here the Comoros start at a greater disadvantage than their immediate rivals. Even if tourism led to a growth in foreign-exchange earnings, it is doubtful if it would lead to much employment for the tens of thousands of Comorians now in need of wages.

The Comoros are not the only island group facing the converging pressures of population growth and limited land space. A similar set of problems faces the rulers of the smaller Caribbean islands and Cape Verde, to name but two. In each case emigration used to act as a major relief until, with the onset of independence and world economic recession, the emigrants were no longer welcome. Like the citizens of Cape Verde and the West Indies, the Comorians have been doubly crippled by a colonialism that left their country economically backward and now deprives them of opportunities to emigrate to earn a living within the mother economy.

The future must contain vigorous government measures to limit population growth and conserve the ecology of the islands. Beyond that, the Comoros must seek a place in some wider economic grouping, however politically unpalatable that may be. The opportunities in that direction are discussed in the final chapter.

NOTES

1. For a modern description of the peasant economy see Claude Robineau, *Société et économie d'Anjouan* (Paris: ORSTOM, 1966), chap. 2.
2. Jules Repiquet, *Le sultanat d'Anjouan* (Paris: Challanel, 1901), says that one of the first acts of the French protectorate administration in Anjouan was to persuade the sultan to take action against deforestation.
3. H. Isnard, "L'archipel des Comores," *Les cahiers d'outre-mer* 21 (1953), p. 15.
4. Thierry Flobert, *Les Comores*, Travaux et Memoires de la Faculté de Droit et de Science Politique d'Aix-Marseille No. 24 (Marseille: Marseille P.U., 1974), pp. 257–260; Isnard, "L'archipel des Comores," p. 13–16.

5. Isnard, "L'archipel des Comores," p. 16; and Robineau, *Société et économie d'Anjouan*, chap. 3.

6. Figures in Isnard, "L'archipel des Comores," pp. 18–19; Claude Robineau, *Approche sociologique des Comores* (Paris: ORSTOM, 1962), p. 12, cyclostyled; Robineau, *Société et économie d'Anjouan*, pp. 45, 176.

7. Isnard, "L'archipel des Comores," p. 13.

8. These figures are derived from Robineau, *Société et économie d'Anjouan*, p. 43; and Claude Gaspart, "The Comoro Islands since Independence: an Economic Appraisal," in Section II of the ICIOS Conference (Perth, 1979), appendix 1.

9. Thierry Mantoux, "Notes socio-économiques sur l'archipel des Comores," *Revue française d'études politiques africaines* 100 (1974), p. 42. Also Jean-Marie Boisson, "L'économie des Comores," *Annuaire des pays de l'Océan Indien* (1975), pp. 323–343.

10. G. Bastian, "La situation économique des Comores," *Madagascar: revue de géographie* 2 (1963), p. 76.

11. Ibid., p. 67.

12. H. Chagnoux and A. Haribou, *Les Comores* (Paris: Presses Universitaires de France, 1980), p. 93.

13. Gaspart, "The Comoro Islands since Independence," p. 9. In 1979 domestic rice production was worth 222.0 million CFA compared with imports worth 1091.7 million CFA. In other words domestic production amounted to only just over 20 percent of imports. The same year food imports made up 35 percent of the total import bill. World Bank, *The Comoros: Current Economic Situation and Prospects* (Washington, D.C.: World Bank, 1983), pp. 55, 67.

14. Ibid., p. 10.

15. For a detailed study of the fishing boats and the industry as a whole see Geneviève Giraud, "Etude morphologique de la pirogue à balancier aux Comores et dans l'ouest de l'Océan Indien" (Masters Thesis, University of Paris, 1973).

16. Gaspart, "The Comoro Islands since Independence," p. 10; World Bank, *Comoros*, p. 138. Other estimates put the potential much lower, e.g., Chagnoux and Haribou, *Les Comores*, p. 119.

17. Isnard, "L'archipel des Comores," pp. 10–13.

18. This discussion is based on an article on the scent industry published in the cyclostyled Comorian government publication *Info'Comore* 12 (1973) entitled "Les huiles essentielles aux Comores."

19. Robineau, *Approche sociologique des Comores*, p. 10. In two articles published in *Le Monde*, December 1, 2, 1972, Philippe Decraene asserted that 85 percent of vanilla exports were controlled by just three companies while five controlled the export of ylang-ylang essence.

20. Mantoux, "Notes socio-économiques sur l'archipel des Comores," p. 46.

21. Chagnoux and Haribou, *Les Comores*, pp. 100–101; in 1980 there were 451 km (281.8 miles) of paved road complete. World Bank, *Comoros*, p. 26.

22. Flobert, *Les Comores*, p. 233; in 1980 one of the cargo vessels leased by the Comorian government was confined to territorial waters for fear of being impounded for debt. World Bank, *Comoros*, p. 25.

23. Chagnoux and Haribou, *Les Comores*, p. 102.

24. Flobert, *Les Comores*, pp. 288–289.

25. For foreign trade of the Comoros see G. Lavau, "Les Comores," *La revue de Madagascar*, April (1934), pp. 129–130; Bastian, "La situation économique

des Comores," pp. 74–78; Gaspart, "The Comoro Islands since Independence,"
pp. 12–13; Boisson, "L'économie des Comores," p. 333.

26. Gaspart, "The Comoro Islands since Independence," p. 13.

27. Figures derived from ibid., p. 13.

28. Mantoux, "Notes socio-économiques sur l'archipel des Comores," p. 49.

29. John Carvel, "The Economy," Seychelles Supplement in the *Guardian*, June 4, 1982.

30. Chagnoux and Haribou, *Les Comores*, p. 121; Flobert, *Les Comores*, p. 282; World Bank, *Comoros*, p. 23.

31. Mantoux, "Notes socio-économiques sur l'archipel des Comores," p. 45.

32. A sympathetic account of the Soilih revolution is contained in Chagnoux and Haribou, *Les Comores*, chap. 5; a slightly more sceptical, but still fair, account is given in "Comoro Islands," *Africa Contemporary Record* 10 (1977–1978), pp. B188–B196.

33. See reports entitled "Comoro Islands," *Africa Contemporary Record* 10 (1977–1978) and 11 (1978–1979).

34. See details in "Comoro Islands," *Africa Contemporary Record* 12 (1979–1980), pp. B168–B176; *Africa Research Bulletin* 16 (1979) and 17 (1980); and World Bank, *Comoros*, pp. 4–16, 34.

35. "Comoro Islands," *Africa Contemporary Record* 10 (1977–1978), p. B195.

36. Chagnoux and Haribou, *Les Comores*, p. 121, quotes an estimate that forest in 1974 had been reduced to 46,000 hectares, (177.6 square miles), half what was necessary for the conservation of the soil and the islands' moisture.

6

The Comoros and the World Community

Between 1975 and 1978 the Comoro islanders were cast adrift by their leaders and were able to experiment with complete independence. They put to the test the theories of those who wanted the islands to pursue policies of self-sufficiency and to find friends other than France in the international community. In 1978 they were rudely returned to their old position as a French protectorate, but this time with the difference that the political opposition was not able to offer much in the way of a credible alternative. Moreover, going it alone could no longer be represented as the only alternative to French protection. The growth of the rivalry between the Soviet Union and the United States in the Indian Ocean meant that even if they won freedom from French dominance, the Comoros would be drawn into the sphere of influence of one or the other of the superpowers.

In 1970 the Indian Ocean was not a major theater of cold-war activity. The old colonial powers, Britain and France, were still dominant: the British with bases in the Gulf and Singapore and a colonial regime in the Seychelles; the French with their military base at Diego Suarez in Madagascar and with colonies in Djibouti, Réunion, and the Comoros. The only other military power active in the Indian Ocean was Iran. During the 1970s Britain and Iran, for different reasons, largely faded from the scene. Britain gave up its Gulf bases in 1971 and made the Seychelles independent in 1976, and the fall of the shah in 1979 and the subsequent war with Iraq ended any significant Iranian presence. France lost its base at Diego Suarez after President Tsiranana fell from power in 1972, although the decline of its influence was much less marked than the decline of Britain's.

As the old powers departed, the Soviet Union and the United States increasingly filled the vacuum. The Americans had leased the island of Diego Garcia from Britain as early as 1965, and the Russians had cultivated friendships in South Yemen (formerly British Aden) and

Waterfront of Moroni: The slopes of the Karthala Volcano behind

Somalia. In 1975 the Russians were expelled from Somalia, but in the *renversement des alliances* that followed they were able to build a base at Massawa on the Red Sea coast of Eritrea. Both powers then proceeded to introduce a formidable naval presence in the Indian Ocean of at least thirty warships apiece, backed by strike units for land operations. The U.S. buildup accelerated after the fall of the shah.[1]

Most observers have concluded that the Americans and the Russians are principally concerned with watching each other and that neither side has tried, and certainly neither has succeeded, in creating a system of client-states in the Indian Ocean. The United States had friends in Saudi Arabia, the Gulf, Kenya, and Somalia, but the friendships were distant ones, and the most dependent state in that region, Oman, seemed more anxious to remain a client of Britain than of the United States. Russia, it is true, had client states in South Yemen and Ethiopia, the latter heavily dependent on Russian military support, but found few other allies, and attempts in the early 1980s to form close ties with the Seychelles, if indeed there were such attempts, were not successful. For the most part, littoral states of the Indian Ocean remained outside the power blocs, and it is this circumstance that enabled France to play such an effective role.

As long as France retains its presence in the Indian Ocean, the Comoros are likely to remain part of its informal empire. However, the exact nature and purpose of this French Indian Ocean presence is difficult to define. French airforce units and a large garrison were installed in Djibouti as a support for the friendly regime placed in power there at the time of independence. In 1981 the garrison there amounted to 6,500 legionnaires. The island of Réunion has become a full French department and a bastion of right-wing creole power. The Réunionais leaders press strongly for departmental status to be granted also to Mayotte, partly in order to increase France's commitment to remain in the Indian Ocean and partly so that that island can become an outlet for Réunion's economic enterprise. Mayotte ostensibly forms the third component of this Indian Ocean military presence and also has a unit of the French Foreign Legion as its permanent garrison.[2]

The French military and naval presence in the Indian Ocean is sometimes explained as vital for the protection of the route taken by the oiltankers from the Gulf on their way to Europe and the United States. Every day supertankers pass through the Mozambique Channel on their way to the Cape of Good Hope, and the Comoro Islands are strategically placed to protect, or alternatively to interfere with, their passage. France's continued possession of the uninhabited islands that lie along the eastern side of the channel also demonstrates a concern for the channel's safety. The most important of these islands are the Iles Glorieuses, the Bassas da India, Europa, and João da Nova islands, which were detached from the government of Madagascar together with the Comoro Islands in 1960. They have been retained under full French sovereignty, and a small garrison has even been placed on the Iles Glorieuses. Both Madagascar and the Comoros claim these islands. In 1979 the OAU publicly supported Madagascar's position, and France was quite happy to see its client, Ahmed Abdullah, advance rival claims on the part of the Comoros in order to muddy the waters of OAU diplomacy.[3]

Yet the thesis that France is building a massive military and naval presence in the Indian Ocean cannot really be substantiated in the face of the obvious lack of any modern installations in the Mozambique area or of any policy to develop these French territories in ways that would make them significant in an Indian Ocean war. The Iles Glorieuses have not been turned into France's "Diego Garcia," and for all the French talk about the strategic value of Mayotte, they have not invested in port facilities in the lagoon or even in extensions to the little airstrip since Mayotte declared itself French in 1975. French warships visiting Mayotte still have to anchor offshore and use lighters. Since the restoration of Abdullah the French have signed a bilateral treaty that allows them to make use of the facilities, such as they are, on the other three islands, but none of the other islands has a deepwater port or any modern repair or handling equipment.

Probably France's position can best be described as preemptive. The islands of the Mozambique Channel *might* one day be important and certainly they *could* be used by some power to interfere with international shipping lanes. Moreover, oil or some other raw material *might* be found in the area. Better that France should keep its options open and retain its territorial claims and the influence that these give it in Indian Ocean affairs. Furthermore, France's presence in the Indian

Ocean does give it a capacity for limited political intervention. The overthrow of Soilih's regime in 1978 is a clear example; another is the promptness with which the French were able to dispatch aid to President René of the Seychelles in August 1982. Such political intervention, very low-key at present, will nevertheless not have gone unnoticed by those whom France is trying to woo into the newly conceived French "commonwealth."

After granting independence to almost all its colonies in the early 1960s, France retained much closer formal and informal ties with them than did Britain with its colonies. These links took the form of a French military presence and of close economic ties, with French aid sustaining many of their economies. In the late 1970s, however, this neo-colonial empire began to assume a clearer and more positive form. The OAU was visibly weakening as a way of securing African political cooperation, and in 1982 the issue of the Western Sahara so split the organization that it was unable to meet at all. As the OAU disintegrated, the Franco-African summits assumed increasing importance. Starting simply as meetings of France with its African clients, the summits grew to include the former Belgian territories (also Francophone) and, more recently, the former Portuguese colonies, whose own mutual cooperation had distinctly weakened since independence and particularly since the rift between Guinea-Bissau and Cape Verde in 1980. Former British colonies also began to be involved, with Gambia and Sierre Leone, as well as the partly Francophone Mauritius and Seychelles, attending the 1982 meeting.[4]

It is strongly denied in Paris that the Franco-African summits are a challenge to the OAU, but the very vigor of the denials is a clear sign that the reality is to the contrary and that these meetings are rapidly becoming one of the most influential forums for the discussion of African problems. In 1979 the idea of a French "commonwealth"— Communauté Organique—was proposed, to include not only Francophone African territories but those in the Pacific and Americas as well. Therefore, French activity in the Indian Ocean and determination to hold onto Mayotte appear as part of a wider strategy for maintaining France as a world power alongside the United States and Russia.

However, if the Comoro Islands have become largely captives of France and French interests, they are not wholly so. The Soilih years did teach the Comorians some of the advantages of widening the islands' economic and political contacts; and relations cultivated by Soilih with Tanzania, China, the Arab countries, and the EEC have not by any means been abandoned since 1978. China and Nigeria established diplomatic missions in the Comoros, whereas before 1975 the only official contacts with other states had been through the French high commission. However, the two principal directions in which the Comoros have begun to look for additional aid and cooperation are to their immediate neighbors in Africa and to the Gulf states.

As a country with an entirely Muslim population there are clearly opportunities for the Comoros to build up relations with the Arab world. The 1970s were a decade of rapid growth of the economies of the Gulf states, and many Comorians went there as migrant workers just as previously they had gone to Madagascar and East Africa. At the same time some of the Arab states, notably Saudi Arabia, Kuwait, and Abu Dhabi, were forward in providing loans to the Comoros for such things as telephone installations and airport extensions. The Arab Development Bank for Africa also lent the Comoros money. In September 1980 Ahmed Abdullah visited Kuwait and in 1982, Libya; and the further development of relations with Arab states is clearly one option for Comorian policy-makers.[5] However, the basis for close ties with the Arab world may not be as firm as would at first appear. The Comorian people are Swahili in culture, not Arab, and few, if any, of them speak or understand Arabic. The islands have a marked surplus of population, but in supplying unskilled labor they are competing with India and Pakistan, with which the Gulf states have agreements. Moreover, with the growth of extreme Islamic policies in Iran and Pakistan, the Comoros' recent attempt to rid themselves of some of the traditional Islamic practices may be out of step with the rest of the Muslim world.

The Comoros have had traditional and historic ties with their immediate neighbors, Tanzania, Madagascar, and Mozambique. These might easily be turned into present-day alliances and spheres of coop-eration. However, the circumstances of Abdullah's restoration, the in-tervention of French mercenaries, and the obvious continuation of political control from Paris have estranged the archipelago's closest neighbors. Abdullah is not welcome in Madagascar, Tanzania, or Mozambique, although all three are closely involved in Indian Ocean affairs. Never-theless, the Comoros have joined such organizations as the African Parliamentary Union and the Eastern and Southern Africa Management Institute. Significantly, they have also become involved in discussions for setting up a preferential trade area in eastern Africa that could lead to the emergence of some kind of regional common market.[6]

Rather fewer links seem to have been built with other Indian Ocean states. Mauritius, the Seychelles, and Réunion share with the Comoros a background of French colonization and plantation capitalism that has left a legacy of underdevelopment and overpopulation. However, the very similarity of the problems faced by these states makes them rivals as much as partners—rivals in the development of their almost identical assets, such as tropical agriculture and tourism. In the early 1980s it was French policy to cultivate good relations with the Seychelles and Mauritius while strengthening direct political control in Réunion and the Comoros.[7] In spite of a long-standing dispute with France over the status of Tromelin Island, Mauritius, in particular, showed every sign of wanting to welcome France as a close ally and protector. If France's "island policy" matures further, the Comoros may well be drawn by

France itself into closer cooperation with the other tiny Indian Ocean states. Cooperation is indeed the only way such small communities can retain a reasonable degree of independence while at the same time developing the amenities and infrastructure of a modern state. Fields such as fishery research, technical training, higher education, tourism, and health and tropical research are ideal for such cooperative efforts. Ultimately, national security itself might even be attained by cooperation.

The search for security and neutrality in the Indian Ocean is not a new ideal. Demilitarization of the Indian Ocean, at least as far as the great powers are concerned, has been talked about since the late 1960s. In the early 1980s the idea gained extra impetus from the intensification of great-power rivalry and from the fact that Mauritius, the Seychelles, and Madagascar were able to link the issue to their territorial claims. A neutralization of the Indian Ocean and the creation there of a "zone of peace," as the current political expression has it, would involve a removal of French and U.S. bases. The obstacles to the return of Diego Garcia to the Seychelles, Tromelin to Mauritius, and the Iles Glorieuses to Madagascar would then be removed. Any impediment to Mayotte rejoining the Comoros would also be removed. In July 1982 a so-called Indian Ocean Commission was formed linking the Seychelles, Mauritius, and Madagascar. The Comoros would seem to be natural partners in this search for neutrality. It is significant that when Said Ali Kemal, the Comorian ambassador in Paris, resigned in order to lead a movement in opposition to Ahmed Abdullah in 1981, part of his platform was to demand that the Comoros cultivate closer links with Madagascar and support the idea of the "zone of peace."[8]

It is difficult to conclude, however, that the immediate future of the Comoros lies with anyone other than the one who pays the bills and keeps the leaky economy of the archipelago afloat. As Prince Said Ibrahim pointed out as long ago as the 1960s, "There is no political independence without economic independence." The Comoros are not alone in being small, desperately poor, and only nominally independent. Their position, for example, begs comparison with the Cape Verde Islands on the other side of Africa. The problem of combining security and development with a genuine degree of independence may in the end prove to be without solution, but the only chance of achieving it will be through regional cooperation with other states of a like size. If Comorian politicians would study the history of their islands before the French occupation, they might learn something of the commercial and political interdependence that once existed in the area of the western Indian Ocean.

NOTES

1. P. M. Allen, "The Indian Ocean: a New Era of Conflict or a Zone of Peace?" *Africa Contemporary Record* 13 (1980–81), pp. A72–79.

2. Michael Field, "Self-interest in the Comoros," *Daily Telegraph*, October 29, 1974; J-P. Gomane, "France and the Indian Ocean," in L. W. Bowman and I. Clark, eds., *The Indian Ocean in Global Politics* (Boulder: Westview Press, 1981), pp. 189–203.

3. OAU Council of Ministers, session held in Monrovia, July 1979, resolution 732 (xxxiii), "On the Islands of Glorieuses, Juan de Nova, Europa and Bassas da India," printed in *Africa Contemporary Record* 12 (1979–80), p. C13.

4. Gomane, "France and the Indian Ocean"; Claude Wauthier, "France in Africa: President Giscard d'Estaing's Ambitious Diplomacy," *Africa Contemporary Record* 12 (1979–80), pp. A120–127; Claude Wauthier, "France and Africa in 1980: a Year of Minor Setbacks," *Africa Contemporary Record* 13 (1980–81), pp. A168–176.

5. Details in *Africa Research Bulletin*, 1980, 1981, 1982.

6. *Africa Research Bulletin* (1982), Economic, Financial and Technical Series, June–July 1982.

7. "Seychelles: a Special Report," *Guardian*, June 4, 1982.

8. Allen, "The Indian Ocean: a New Area of Conflict of a Zone of Peace?"; G. W. Shepherd, "Demilitarization Proposals for the Indian Ocean," in Bowman and Clark, eds., *The Indian Ocean in Global Politics*, pp. 223–247.

Bibliographical Essay

Even for readers of French there is very little information available in print on the Comoro Islands. Except for some studies made of the Karthala Volcano, little research of any kind was carried on before the 1950s, and it has been only since the mid-1960s that a number of serious works have appeared. Unfortunately, with one exception, these have either appeared in obscure publications or have remained in cyclostyled format with a circulation only among those with the expertise to discover their existence. Not until 1980, when the excellent booklet *Les Comores* by H. Chagnoux and Ali Haribou appeared, was there any generally available published account of the islands.

Nevertheless, for those with the time and inclination to pursue elusive academic publications and defunct journals, there has always been a massive amount of primary material available. English readers might start by reading Barbara Dubins, "The Comoro Islands: a Bibliographical Essay" and follow this by consulting the exhaustive bibliography attached to her thesis. From these it will be clear that there is a large amount of material in English for the seventeenth, eighteenth, and nineteenth centuries when the islands were a regular port of call for English ships bound for India. Indeed, almost every account of voyages made to the East contains a description of the islands. The fullest of these is undoubtedly that of Sir William Jones, but the volumes of the Hakluyt Society have preserved many other accounts in reasonably accessible form.

After the French had secured control of the islands at the end of the nineteenth century, there were a number of important works written that reflected the intense public interest in all things African at that period. The earliest and certainly the best of these was A. L. Gevrey's *Essai sur les Comores*, but the list might include the important works of Repiquet, Vienne, and Du Plantier. This period of interest in the islands was crowned with the publication of a massive study of the history, geography, and ethnology of the archipelago by A. Völtzkow. This work

131

has been little used by subsequent writers and is very difficult to obtain, but among other reasons, it deserves to be better known for its exhaustive bibliography of all aspects of the islands up to 1914.

From 1914 until World War II the Comoros were largely forgotten. No research was carried out and this lack of interest is reflected in the extreme paucity of publications during this period. For instance, two of the books published at this time, Fontoynant's *La Grande Comore* and Faurec's *Archipel des Sultans Batailleurs,* are a muddle of hearsay, legends, and a fictionalized version of events based on a repetition of earlier writers.

After the war interest in the islands was stimulated again by the sensational discovery of the coelacanth, and a number of scientific expeditions visited the archipelago, resulting in the publication of studies of the Comorian fauna and geology. However, it was only in the mid-1960s that serious academic study of the islands was really launched. In 1964 Jean Gorse's bibliography appeared, but unfortunately only in cyclostyled format. Meanwhile, Claude Robineau published three works on the history, society, and economy of Anjouan, works quite indispensable for the modern study of the island but sadly long out of print and hard to obtain. Also in the 1960s, Georges and Geneviève Boulinier began their investigations into the culture of the islands. It is impossible to overemphasize the contribution they have made toward placing the study of the Comoros on a sound academic footing. They have pioneered the study of the music, song, and traditions of the islands, have updated the bibliography, and have organized a stream of academic articles on aspects of the islands' ethnology.

In 1972 Barbara Dubins completed her thesis on the nineteenth-century history of the islands. Regrettably, this meticulously researched thesis was never published and is not, therefore, readily available for the casual reader. The other modern historian of the islands has been Jean Martin, whose articles, mostly on the nineteenth-century history of the archipelago, began to be written in the 1960s. However, it was only in 1974 that the first general study of the islands appeared, with the publication of Thierry Flobert's *Les Comores.* Unfortunately, this academic publication appeared only as a photoprinted typescript and was not widely known until publicized by the appearance of Chagnoux and Haribou's booklet in 1980. For the period of the 1970s and 1980s the essays published annually in the *Africa Contemporary Record* are an important source for English readers, although it was not until about 1975 that these essays provided anything more than the most sketchy outline of the archipelago's affairs. The other major commentary on contemporary affairs is provided by the *Annuaire des Pays de l'Océan Indien,* which is published in Aix en Provence, and a weekly digest of Indian Ocean news, the *Indian Ocean Newsletter,* which began to be produced in Paris in 1981.

There are still major fields of investigation that have scarcely begun, and others that never will. The burning of the government archives by

Soilih's followers in 1977 place a limit on the amount of research that can ever by undertaken on the modern history of the islands. In a different category is the rich literature of the islanders themselves, first discovered in the nineteenth century but only now in the process of publication. The archaeology of the Comoros has not progressed very far. The few exploratory studies that have been made merely highlight the potential of this field for research. In particular, a number of ruined town sites, notably at Sima and the old town above Numa Choa on Mohéli, are worthy of investigation.

SELECT BIBLIOGRAPHY
(With special reference to works in English)

Bibliographies

Dubins, Barbara. "The Comoro Islands: a Bibliographical Essay." *African Studies Bulletin* 12 (1969): 131–137.
Boulinier, Georges, and Boulinier-Giraud, Geneviève. "Volcanisme et traditions populaires à la Grande Comore." *Asie du sud-est et monde insulindien* 7 (1976): 45–71 (Bibliography, pp. 62–71).
Boulinier, Georges. "Thèses et mémoires universitaires sur les Comores." *Journal des Africanistes* 49 (1979): 173–177.
Gorse, Jean. *Territoire des Comores: bibliographie.* Paris: BDPA, 1964. Cyclostyled.
Völtzkow, A. *Die Comoren,* vol. 1, pt. 1, of *Reise in Ost-Afrika.* Stuttgart, 1914 (Bibliography, pp. 356–380).

Geography and Natural History

Benson, C. W. "The Birds of the Comoro Islands." *Ibis* 103b (1960): 55–106.
Esson, J., Flower, M., Strong, D., Lupton, B., and Wadsworth, W. "Geology of the Comores Archipelago, Western Indian Ocean." *Geological Magazine* 107 (1970): 549–557.
Prosperi, F. *A Vanished Continent.* London: Hutchinson, 1957.
Smith, J.L.B. *Old Fourlegs; the Story of the Coelacanth.* London: Pan Books, 1958.
Strong, D., and Jacquot, F. "The Karthala Caldera, Grande Comore." *Bulletin Volcanologique* 34 (1971): 663–680.

History

Anon. "A Visit to the Island of Johanna." *United Service Journal* 1 (1830): 144–152.
Dubins, Barbara. "A Political History of the Comoro Islands 1795–1886." Doctoral thesis. Boston: 1972.
Gevrey, A. L. *Essai sur les Comores.* Pondichery: A. Saligny, 1870.
Graham, G. S. *Great Britain in the Indian Ocean 1810–1850.* Oxford: Clarendon Press, 1967.
Jones, Sir William. "Remarks on the Island of Hinzuan, or Johanna." *Asiatic Researches.* London, 1807: vol. 2, 77–107.
Martin, Jean. "Les débuts du protectorat et la revolte servile de 1891 dans l'île d'Anjouan." *Revue française d'histoire d'outre-mer* 1 trimestre (1973): 45–85.

Martin, Jean. "L'affranchissement des esclaves de Mayotte décembre 1846–juillet 1847." *Cahiers d'études africaines* 16 (1976): 207–233.
Newitt, M.D.D. "The Comoro Islands in Indian Ocean Trade before the Nineteenth Century." Proceedings of the ICIOS Conference, Perth, 1979. Section III.
Repiquet, Jules. *Le sultanat d'Anjouan.* Paris: Challanel, 1901.
Vienne, Emile. *Notice sur Mayotte et les Comores.* Paris, 1900.
Wright, H. T., and Kus, Susan. "Notes préliminaires sur une reconnaissance archéologique de l'île de Mayotte (archipel des Comores)." *Asie du sud-est et monde insulindien* 7 (1976): 123–135.

Economy

Bastian, G. "La situation économique des Comores." Madagascar: *Revue de Géographie* 2 (1963): 61–83.
Mantoux, Thierry. "Notes socio-économiques sur l'archipel des Comores." *Revue française d'études politiques africaines* 100 (1974): 41–60.
Gaspart, Claude. "The Comoro Islands since Independence: an Economic Appraisal." Proceedings of the ICIOS Conference, Perth, 1979. Section II.
Robineau, Claude. *Société et économie d'Anjouan.* Paris: ORSTOM, 1966.

Society

Hébert, J-C. "Fêtes agraires dans l'île d'Anjouan." *Journal de la société des africanistes* 30 (1960): 101–116.
Martin, Jean. "Les notions des clans, nobles et notables: leur impact dans la vie politique comorienne d'aujourd'hui." *L'Afrique et l'Asie* 81–82 (1968): 39–63.
Robineau, Claude. *Approche sociologique des Comores.* Paris: ORSTOM, 1962.
Shepherd, G. M. "Two Marriage Forms in the Comoro Islands: an Investigation." *Africa* 47 (1977): 344–359.
World Bank. *The Comoros: Current Economic Situation and Prospects.* Washington, D.C.: World Bank, 1983.

Politics

Africa Contemporary Record. 12 vols. New York and London: Africana Publication Corporation, 1968–1980.
Bourde, André. "The Comoro Islands: Problems of a Microcosm." *Journal of Modern African Studies* 3 (1965): 91–102.
Martin, Jean. "L'archipel des Comores," *Revue française d'études politiques africaines* 44 (1968): 6–39.
Ostheimer, John. "The Politics of Comorian Independence." In John Ostheimer, ed., *The Politics of the Western Indian Ocean.* New York: Praeger, 1975. 73–101.
Saint–Alban, C. "Les partis politiques comoriens." *Revue française d'études politiques africaines.* October (1973): 76–91.

General

Chagnoux, H., and Haribou, Ali. *Les Comores.* Paris: Presses Universitaires de France, 1980.
Flobert, Thierry. *Les Comores.* Travaux et Mémoires de la Faculté de Droit et de Science Politiques d'Aix-Marseille, No. 24. Aix-Marseilles: Marseilles P.U., 1974.

Index

About the Book and Author

THE COMORO ISLANDS
Struggle Against Dependency in the Indian Ocean
Malyn Newitt

Occupying a strategic position at the head of the Mozambique Channel, the four islands of the Comoro archipelago lie between Madagascar and Mozambique and have shared the cultural and economic evolution of both regions. The primarily Islamic population has traditionally had strong cultural, commercial, and political ties with East Africa, although the easternmost island, Mayotte, has tended to look more toward Madascar. Mayotte was occupied by France in the 1840s as a counterweight to the British in Zanzibar, and from there French influence dominated the entire archipelago. The French developed the islands as plantations, and most of the best land was expropriated by French companies; the Islamic aristocracy secured control of much of the rest and struck up a working alliance with the French authorities. In the 1970s, politics in the Comoros became explosive, and three of the islands declared their independence from France to form the Comoro state. Mayotte chose to remain under French administration.

In this first book in English about the Comoros, Dr. Newitt explores the islands' historical and contemporary links with Africa and the political dilemma that faces them and their French "big brother" in the postcolonial period. Most critical among the problems confronting the islands, he emphasizes, are overpopulation and the competing claims of export crops and subsistence agriculture for the very limited land resources. The Comoros have already experienced one abortive popular revolution, and unless the political and economic contradictions can be resolved, Dr. Newitt predicts, further revolutionary movements appear likely.

Dr. Malyn Newitt is senior lecturer in history at the University of Exeter and has also taught at the University of Rhodesia. He is the author of *Portuguese Settlement on the Zambesi* (1973) and *Portugal in Africa: The Last Hundred Years* (1981).